EAT What You Love!

Southern LiteStyle Cooking

with

Stacey Browning Pardue, LDN, RD

Edited by
Leeanne Bamburg Bordelon

Photographer Kevin Hawkins is a Louisiana native with a Masters degree in Business Administration from Louisiana Tech University. His work has been featured on several cookbooks and in numerous publications. He serves on the Board of Directors of the Professional Photographers of Louisiana. Kevin has been featured in the General Collection of Awards for the Professional Photographers of America and has also been awarded a Fuji Masterpiece Award. Examples of his work can be found at his web site: www.hawkinsphoto.com.

■■■■■■■■■■■■■

Victor David Cascio, table designer, is co-owner of The Chateau Restaurant in Monroe, Louisiana. He has traveled extensively in the United States and in Europe, where he was once a guest of Queen Elizabeth. Victor writes a weekly social column and a monthly feature on food and table settings for the *Monroe News-Star*. He is also a regular contributor to *Delta Style* magazine. For the past 18 years, Victor has hosted a television show titled *Holidays with Victor*, which airs on CBS affiliate KNOE-TV in Monroe. Victor is married to Marie Fruge Cascio. He has three sons and four grandsons.

Outdoor photographs taken at the homes of Mr. and Mrs. Joe and Ann Ledoux and Mr. and Mrs. Duane and Gail Humphries, all of Monroe. Creative and production assistance by Martha Murphy, Randy Dark, Linda Peevy, Jama Brown, Jill Menzina, Janet Wyatt, Erika Myers, Jennifer Teat, Gene Mcgaha, G.C. & Company of Jonesboro, Lewis of Ruston, and Kaye's Foods.

1st Printing   December 2001   5,000 copies
2nd Printing   February 2002   7,000 copies

Copyright © 2001
ISBN # 1-931294-21-6
Cookbook Resources, LLC, Highland Village, Texas

Manufactured by

cookbook
≈*resources*

Cookbook Resources, LLC
541 Doubletree Drive • Highland Village, Texas 75077
972-317-0245
Toll-Free Orders: 866/229-2665
www.cookbookresources.com

DEDICATION

This book is dedicated to my patient, supportive husband
and our three beautiful and healthy children.
When I look at you, I realize just how good God is.

And to the *"Just Ask Stacey"* viewers,
who have faithfully supported me for
eight wonderful years,
this book is for you.

ACKNOWLEDGEMENTS

To my husband, Bubba, who has survived eight years of taste tests, sleepless nights, early mornings, late-night trips to the grocery store, lots of babysitting, and being talked about on TV!

To my #1 assistants, Victoria and Elizabeth-Kate; and to Tré, who has spent much of his first year of life watching me cook! These days will always be precious to me.

To my parents, Paul and Gloria Browning, for raising me in a loving Christian home, and for shaping me into the young woman I am today. I am so grateful!

To my in-laws, Mrs. Judy and Mr. Larry, thank you for accepting me into your family as a daughter, and supporting me in all aspects of my life—from the "college days" to the "baby days."

To Leeanne Bordelon, who has finally made this book a reality. Words cannot express how grateful I am to you for helping me fulfill this dream. No one will ever know the hours you have spent writing and re-writing, typing and re-typing the contents of this book. Thanks to your supportive family—Kevin, Rick, and Rebecca—for allowing you to share your time with me. You are the most productive stay-at-home mom I know, and I am still praying that some of your productivity will rub off on me!

To Kevin Hawkins, whose art of photography has made this book come to life. You have truly added the "icing on the cake!"

To Randy Pruitt of KNOE, who has supported me from the beginning and encouraged me to be myself. To Ed Murphy, who gave me my start in this business and continues to be an invaluable source of advice and encouragement.

To Mrs. Meg Page and Mrs. Iris Fairbanks for going above and beyond the call of duty to manage and file eight years' worth of recipes at the studio!

To my extended family members and friends who have encouraged and helped me along the way. Special thanks to our dear friends Lonnie and Jill Menzina, who have been my cheerleaders throughout this project.

To all of you who have shared your stories, recipes, ideas, and sentiments through the years: I hope this book reflects a little of what you have taught me.

FOREWORD

Passion. In a list of the world's most important words, *passion* is probably in the top ten, somewhere between "dadireallygottago" and "only2shoppingdaystilChristmas." It is our jet propulsion, an internal ignition that rockets us to unforeseen destinations. It is inspiration squared.

We know all about *passion* here in the South. While others worry about mundane things like pre-birth tuition for private pre-school and a pending merger of "Fluorescent Dentures, Inc." and "Hail Yes Hot Sauce!" here below the Mason-Dixon line we prefer to concentrate our *passion* on the important things, like food and high school football. It just comes natural.

About 8 years ago a producer for a Monroe, Louisiana television show was attempting to meet a huge demand for a new cooking segment. Viewers were clamoring for something differing from traditional cooking show fare. *"We want good food, but we don't want fat thighs! We want large portions but we don't want Chef Rolleaux's Exquisite HeadOnFish-Stuffed Avocado, straight from Paris! We love sauces and gravies but hate strokes! HELP!"*

Call it fate, call it destiny. . . whatever. Just days after the decision to begin a search, this particular producer was talking, (er..exercising) at a local hospital-based fitness center (*passionately*, of course) when he noticed a group of people gathered around a young woman. Being the inquisitive sort (OK, nosey) the producer checked it out and discovered the woman to be a professional dietitian and lifestyle educator. She was offering food samples and heart-healthy advice to a crowd ravenous for both. The woman was a natural, breaking down the food substitutions and "phat" grams (aren't all of 'em *Pretty Hot and Tempting*?) to a language even this producer (who *passionately* loved cheeseburgers) could understand. But, and a big but it was—no pun intended—would this pleasant, attractive individual be as big a hit on television as she was in person? And, would she have a *passion* for the challenge ahead?

Not only did Stacey Pardue embrace the opportunity, she brought an honest, vulnerable personality to the airwaves. The show was called "Just Ask Stacey", and it was an instant sensation. Viewers loved her Southern demeanor and down-home manners. She was one of **THEM**.

That was 8 years ago. To this day "Just Ask Stacey" remains the number one source of information on heart-healthy, low-fat cooking and eating in the ArkLaMiss. Thousands upon thousands watch her segment faithfully, and then request copies of the recipes so they can share her *passion*. Her show is a primary reason "*Good Morning ArkLaMiss*" remains the number one television morning show in Northeast Louisiana, and for that I am eternally grateful. Now, about that high school football.

Ed Murphy
Executive Producer
Good Morning ArkLaMiss
KNOE-TV8
Monroe, LA

CONTENTS

Look for these helpful symbols on the recipes in this book:

A 🦐 denotes a Louisiana Favorites recipe.

A 🎁 denotes a Holiday Ideas recipe.

Acknowledgements................................ 4

Foreword 5

Contents 8

Introduction 10

No More Dieting!................................. 13

Fat Facts 17

Guide Your Food Choices with the
    Food Guide Pyramid 18

Change A Little Save a Lot!...................... 19

Ingredients Make a Difference 21

Recipe Modification 22

Surviving Holidays and Other Celebrations 23

Tips for Surviving the Holidays and
    Other Celebrations 25

What is a Serving?............................... 26

Sample Daily Menus 28

APPETIZERS AND BEVERAGES 38

Let The Good Times Roll!

Let the good times roll with these scrumptious starters—
from Spectacular Spinach Dip to a Strawberry Yogurt Smoothie.
Great for entertaining or anytime, these heart-healthy recipes
taste so good you won't believe they are low fat!

SOUPS, SALADS, BREADS AND SIDES 70

Guiltless Family Favorites!

Add versatility to any meal with Deliciously Different Broccoli
Salad, Spicy Apple Muffins, or Cheesy Potato Soup. Served as a
complement to the main course or enjoyed all by themselves,
these easy recipes are sure to please—without piling on the calories!

MAIN DISHES 128

Put It All Together!

Tired of preparing a separate "diet" meal every night? Try these
hearty but healthy main dishes the entire family will love,
like Crawfish Etouffee, Cheesy Chicken Spaghetti,
Fettuccine Alfredo, and Crescent Pizza Pie.

DESSERTS 198

Have Your King Cake and Eat It Too!

Have your King Cake and eat it, too! The only thing sinful about
these desserts is the taste! From Four-Layer Delight to Fudge
Brownies and Lemon Ice Box Pie, discover a new idea or
traditional favorite for any occasion.

Index 305

Order Form 319

INTRODUCTION

Balance, Moderation & Variety —
The Keys to Eating (and Living)
What You Love!

As a registered dietitian, I have counseled hundreds of patients and clients over the years about eating healthy and being fit, and they all ask me the same thing: "Why does it have to be so hard?" Many people have ridden the dietary roller coaster for years, battling discouragement and even despair. Others have grown bored with limited food choices, or just been unable to follow through with their good intentions to exercise and choose healthy foods.

We are living in a fast-paced society that seeks instant solutions. It is no wonder we are disappointed when fad diets and formulas fail. Most of us have learned the hard way that there is no "magic pill" for weight loss. We know that all the supplements in the world are no substitute for healthy eating, and that diet soft drinks don't really cancel out the calories in chocolate cake!

How can we lose weight and keep it off? How can we eat a healthy diet and take care of our bodies without being miserable? How can we know our resolutions will stick?

My approach to nutrition and health is a liberal one. I believe that people are entitled to feel good about themselves no matter what their size or shape. Beyond that, we have to realize that what we put into our bodies daily affects our present and future health.

This book is about lifestyle changes. It is full of tips, recipes, and other information to help you break free from the painful cycle of dieting and disappointment. Unlike traditional plans that restrict and condemn, lifestyle changes put *you* in control. These changes are made gradually, almost effortlessly, until they become so routine you may wonder why you didn't make them years ago.

I present to you three keys I believe are essential to developing a healthy lifestyle. It may come as a surprise to find that many of my suggestions have nothing to do with food. I am convinced that as you evaluate your lifestyle in terms of these three keys, you will realize that their application goes far beyond counting calories.

The first key is **balance**. If there is anything we need in America today, it is balance! The economic prosperity our country has enjoyed during the past few years has changed our definition of success. Technology has encouraged us to fill our time until we are either exhausted or ineffective. To live a balanced lifestyle, we need to define what is really important to us, and arrange our lives and schedules accordingly.

Balance involves making time for family, for spiritual and personal growth, and for rest. The balanced person is aware of the fine line between working hard and working too much. Balance requires that we say "no" to some commitments and "yes" to some. Like so many mothers with small children, I struggle with balance daily!

Balance is being informed about our health, seeing a doctor regularly and performing self-exams and other preventative health measures. In our eating habits, it means that having a piece of pie after lunch is not an excuse to binge the rest of the day. The balanced person knows that a constant menu of junk food and sweets isn't healthy, but neither is totally eliminating certain foods or food groups. Balance allows us to enjoy many of the foods we love if we are willing to make a few changes in their preparation.

Even if we miss our appointment at the gym, balance says we can push the stroller around the block instead or do some sit-ups in front of the television. Balance focuses not on what we *can't* or *didn't* do, but what we *can* and *will* do. Having our lives in balance keeps us from feeling out of control.

The next key is **moderation**, which means "within reasonable limits." We need moderation in our eating habits; for example, the wisdom to choose reasonable portion sizes. (Moderation is eating a few potato chips, but not the entire bag!) We can learn to exercise self-control during holidays and social occasions, which can be great opportunities to eat too much of the wrong things. Depending on our individual health, moderation may involve cutting back or eliminating the consumption of alcohol or cigarettes, or foods with high sodium or sugar content. Moderation involves self-discipline. It is the key to making lifestyle changes stick.

I have learned that I have a hard time using moderation when there are sweets or other goodies in my house. I have trouble eating only one or two of my favorite low fat cookies! Therefore, I don't keep such items on hand all the time. You may find that you need to make a similar decision regarding foods that are especially tempting.

The last key is **variety**. Variety deals with finding new ways to keep lifestyle commitments. It might be changing your exercise routine, trying a new recipe, or planning a family outing. It could be taking the stairs at work, keeping healthy snacks in your desk, or actually eating in the dining room!

The best way I have found to keep my life in balance, use moderation, and have variety in my routine is to do a continual self-inventory. When I feel that one area is lacking, I do whatever it takes to get back on track immediately. You can, too!

As we begin this journey together, it is important to remember all of the blessings in our lives—the non-food reasons we have to celebrate and be thankful. Our families, friends, and the freedoms we enjoy in this country are all sweet reminders of what is truly important.

I believe we can all experience the richness of life without compromising our health. A Louisiana native, I enjoy the cultures, flavors, and festivals that make our state so attractive to residents and tourists alike. The Louisiana Favorites recipes in this cookbook, for example, offer healthier ways to prepare many traditional southern dishes, so we can have our King Cake and eat it, too!

As you explore the rest of this book, resolve to make at least one lifestyle change—right now! Do it for a week or two, and when you feel that it is safely a part of your routine, add another. Without any doubt, I am convinced that slow and steady steps will carry you all the way to your goal.

No More Dieting!

Drop the "t" in the word "diet" and what do you get?

The cycle always begins the same way. We gather our resolve, clear out the refrigerator, and declare, "I'm going on a diet!" Alas, the very thought of being restricted from certain foods is enough to powerfully increase our desire for them. After a few days we start thinking, "I'm just going to *die* if I have to do this one minute longer!" Chocolate chip cookies call to us in our dreams, and one day we eat six of them at an office party. Giving in becomes easier, and we soon discover that instead of losing weight we have actually gained a pound or two! Perhaps this is not a "good" time to diet, we reason. Maybe we will have better luck after the holidays, or after the kids start school, or after we finish that big project at work. Sound familiar?

I always tell my clients that going "on" a diet eventually results in going "off" a diet. However, when we make lifestyle changes instead, allowing ourselves the foods we love *in moderation*, we are far more likely to succeed.

Having spent a great deal of time talking with people about their weight, I have realized that obesity is not just a *food* issue—it is a *lifestyle* issue. "Starvation" diets and other forms of food control may bring about temporary weight loss, but lifestyle changes must be made in order to have long-term success.

Let's look our three principles—balance, moderation, and variety—as they relate specifically to weight loss and health.

When trying to lose weight, it is important to balance the amount of food eaten during the course of a day or even a week. A good rule is to consume no more than one-third of daily calories at any meal. If a meal contains more than one-third of the recommended calorie intake, balance it by eating lighter meals the rest of the day.

For example, if your schedule calls for an early business meeting and a large breakfast (i.e. at a buffet), choose a lighter lunch, like a salad or vegetable plate, to maintain daily calorie intake. Skipping a meal is never a good idea, as it makes us likely to overeat later in the day.

Going out to dinner one evening? Don't starve yourself all day. Have a balanced breakfast, a light lunch, and a small snack so as not to be

ravenous when sitting down to the evening meal. Our brains function better when our stomachs are not completely empty. We need to learn how to manage our own eating habits to be more in control. No one else can make wise decisions for us!

Balance within a week is equally important. Most people who are dieting keep their commitments Monday-Friday, but overindulge on the weekends because they have starved themselves all week. This kind of imbalance will almost never result in significant weight loss, since fat grams do count on the weekends!

Not only must we consider the *amount* of food we eat, but also the *types* of foods, in order to get the nutrients our bodies need. The U.S. Department of Agriculture's Food Guide Pyramid, shown on page 18, is a wonderful tool for achieving balance in daily food choices.

To achieve weight loss, aim for the lowest number of servings in each tier of the pyramid. For example, 6-11 servings are recommended daily from the Breads and Grains group, but someone who is trying to lose weight should eat no more than about six servings. I recommend that my clients distribute their daily calories between three meals and two or three small snacks per day.

Many popular diets recommend severely restricting or even eliminating carbohydrates. I have always encouraged carbohydrate control instead, since I believe it is a strategy all of us can live with.

Understanding balance is vital to remaining in control. The cycle of bingeing and the resulting feelings of guilt and depression are the reasons many people never reach their weight loss goals.

Everyone knows that high-fat and high-calorie foods must be eaten in moderation. What about all the fat free "diet" foods on the market? A common misconception is that fat free products will not cause weight gain. The fact is, those products still contain calories that can put on the pounds.

One summer, a restaurant in my town introduced a frozen dessert made with fat free yogurt. A friend and I were so excited to have a healthy treat that we went every afternoon to get one. One day, though, we happened to pick up a nutrition guide and realized that our "healthy" treat contained more than 500 calories! Our trips were less frequent after that.

Educate yourself about portion sizes and nutritional information. Many restaurants and fast food establishments offer entrees or combination meals that contain enough food for one person for an entire day! The

chart on page 18, lists the portion sizes for many common foods. For more information, request nutritional guides from your favorite restaurants, or check your local bookstore. I keep a booklet in my purse that lists the calorie and fat content of fast foods.

Sweets, baked goods, and other treats are constant downfalls for the dieter. This goes back to my "drop the 't'" analogy discussed earlier. With the exception of people on severely restricted medical diets, I usually advise my clients not to label any food as "forbidden," provided that the food is eaten in moderation. Telling yourself you can never again have a piece of chocolate cake, for example, is a sure way to increase your desire for chocolate cake until it is all you can think about! It is far better to have a small slice of chocolate cake occasionally than to eat an entire chocolate cake in a moment of weakness. (See my Reduced Fat Chocolate Cola Cake recipe on page 220.)

Variety is the last of our three keys and is the "glue" that can hold your plan together. Variety is essential to staying on track and reaching weight loss goals. First, variety is needed in daily menus. Eating a grilled chicken sandwich every day for lunch, for example, will quickly result in boredom. Have a grilled chicken sandwich one day, then follow it with a grilled shrimp salad or a vegetable plate.

My clients have told me that they often prepare a separate "diet" meal for themselves and another for their families. This is not necessary if meals are prepared using my low fat guidelines and substitutions. This cookbook is full of traditional family-pleasing recipes that have been modified to be lower in fat and calories. It may be surprising to discover the wide variety of foods that can be enjoyed with your family while still achieving weight loss. Remember to use moderation in your portion sizes, and follow the other guidelines, especially regarding carbohydrate intake.

Another way to achieve variety in the diet is to pay attention to color. When selecting fruits and vegetables, a good rule is that usually the richer the color, the richer the nutrients. Iceberg lettuce, for example, is considered a free food because it has little nutritional value. Spinach, on the other hand, is packed with vitamins and iron.

When cutting calories to lose weight, try to maximize the calories eaten to give the body the most nutrients. Eat several servings of fruits and vegetables, and use variety in the items selected. Instead of a banana with breakfast, try an orange. A serving of grapes or strawberries has more nutritional value than applesauce or fruit cocktail at snack time. For lunch, order a spinach salad topped with sprouts. At dinner, substitute steamed broccoli and carrots for starchy vegetables like corn

or peas. Eating a variety of fruits and vegetables is a good way to fight disease, add fiber to the diet, and provide the nutrients and antioxidants the body needs.

A good weight loss plan is not complete without attention to proper water intake and exercise. The recommended amount of water is six to eight glasses per day, or 48-64 ounces. I find it easier to follow this guideline when I drink water from 16-ounce or 24-ounce bottles, and space my consumption throughout the day. Water helps provide us with satiety (a feeling of fullness) and is a cleanser to our bodies and organs. When I am having trouble drinking enough water, I use positive self-talk to remind myself of water's benefits. I say, "I'm going to drink this water and flush out all my body's toxins and impurities—and maybe even flush out some extra fat!"

Everyone knows that exercise burns calories and fat, but did you know that it also has a tremendous impact on our physical and mental health? The most important factor in exercise is choosing an activity you enjoy. To have the most benefit, exercise should be aerobic, elevating the heart rate for a specific time and increasing oxygen to the heart and lungs. Some aerobic activities are walking, jogging, biking and swimming. See my next book for a more complete discussion of exercise.

By using balance, moderation, and variety in menus and food choices— combined with water intake and regular exercise—you can break the dieting cycle in your life!

FAT FACTS

Cutting back on the amount of fat in our diet makes sense if we want to take care of our bodies and prevent health problems—especially heart disease. But the information about fat can be confusing. Let's take a look at some simple facts about fat.

Fat comes from three main sources: saturated, polyunsaturated, and monounsaturated. Saturated fat elevates LDL or "bad" cholesterol and is the most harmful to the heart. Found in animal products like meat, cheese, and butter, saturated fat is solid at room temperature. Polyunsaturated fats are found in vegetable oils (corn, soybean, cotton, safflower, etc.) and are slightly better for health, as they remain liquid at room temperature. However, sometimes these fats are hydrogenated, which means they are hardened and used to make products like shortening, stick margarine, crackers, cookies, and potato chips.

Hydrogenated or partially hydrogenated fats are just as dangerous to the heart as saturated fats, so they should be reduced or eliminated whenever possible. When shopping, check for ingredients like "partially hydrogenated vegetable oil" on the labels of processed foods.

Monounsaturated fats have been shown to reduce LDL cholesterol and reduce the risk of heart disease. These fats are found in olive, canola, avocado, and nut oils. Using these fats when preparing recipes is a good alternative to saturated fats.

I think it is important to realize that even though olive and canola oils are better selections, they are still fats and have the same amount of total fat and calories as other vegetable oils. I always think of the time early in my career when I first started counseling patients. When I explained fat facts to a particular client, all he heard was that canola and olive oils are "good fats." After one week of eating every imaginable food fried in the "good oils" the client came back for his weekly weigh-in, only to learn that he had gained three pounds!

The facts about fat are this: some "good fats" may be healthier choices when fat is to be consumed in the daily diet. However, most experts agree that reducing the intake of all fats is the best advice for a healthy heart.

GUIDE YOUR
FOOD CHOICES
WITH THE
USDA
FOOD GUIDE PYRAMID

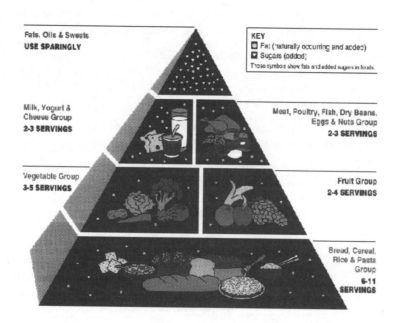

CHANGE A LITTLE ... SAVE A LOT!

Ingredients Make a Difference!
Recipe Modification

If traditional "diet" foods are less than satisfying, try a new strategy! Learn to prepare favorite recipes so that they are lower in fat and calories. Many people believe they must prepare a diet meal for themselves and another for the rest of the family. Not true! With a few easy substitutions, anyone can prepare a delicious *low fat* meal the family will love—and they'll never know the difference!

This cookbook is full of recipes that have already been transformed into healthier versions. But what about all those others in the recipe box? Try the easy tips listed below for modifying favorite dishes.

When evaluating a recipe, ask yourself these questions in terms of reducing fat and calories: Which ingredients can be substituted? Which can be reduced? Which can be completely eliminated?

Substituting healthier versions of original ingredients is my favorite way to modify recipes. The abundance of reduced fat and fat free products on the market makes it easy. Substitute low fat or skim milk products for whole milk products. Use low fat varieties of ricotta and mozzarella cheese when preparing recipes. Reduced fat or fat free versions of sour cream, cream cheese, and mayonnaise can be used in recipes. Low fat or nonfat yogurt is also a good substitute for these items when preparing salads, dips, and sauces.

Tried a fat free product (i.e. cheese) and were not pleased with the results? Don't give up! Next time, try the reduced fat version instead. I have found that some fat free items work well in recipes, but others need a small amount of fat to achieve the desired taste and consistency.

Whenever possible, substitute products like whole wheat pasta, brown rice, and whole wheat flour when preparing recipes. Serve salads and spreads with raw vegetables and low fat or whole wheat crackers. Use fresh fruit instead of canned, and fresh vegetables when they are available.

19

Reducing the fat in recipes may mean literally cutting it in half, which means a significant reduction in calories. If a recipe calls for ½ cup margarine, use only ¼ cup. This can save as many as 480 calories! Use lean cuts of meat and trim any visible fat. Brown meat in a tiny bit of oil, or none at all. Rely on nonstick cookware or cooking spray instead; both are also great to use when sautéing vegetables.

For sauces and dressings, use low-calorie bases (vinegar, mustard, tomato juice, fat free bouillon) instead of high-calorie ones like creams, fats, oils, and mayonnaise. Chill soups, stews, gumbos, and sauces before serving and lift off congealed fat. This saves about 100 calories per tablespoon of fat removed.

Nuts are often a big source of fat in salads and desserts. The amount called for can usually be reduced by one-third to one-half. Try toasting the nuts to give added flavor. Sugar in recipes can also be reduced by about one-fourth to one-third. Added to baked goods, cinnamon, vanilla, ginger, and nutmeg give the impression of sweetness. More than ever before, sugar substitutes today offer a variety of food choices for diabetics. For those on low-sodium diets, the amount of salt in recipes can be reduced by at least one-half.

It may be possible to eliminate some ingredients completely when preparing recipes. Pay attention to toppings, dressings, and garnishes, as they can add significant calories and fat to recipes. Ingredients that are used for texture only can often be omitted. For example, I once prepared a fruit salad that called for pecans and pineapple tidbits. Figuring that the pineapple would add plenty of texture to the salad, I left out the pecans. Without compromising the taste of the salad, I eliminated the fat and significantly reduced the calories.

Use the charts on the following pages as a guide for modifying recipes. Substituting, reducing, and eliminating ingredients can help you and your family eat what you love!

CHANGE A LITTLE ...
SAVE A LOT

Ingredients Make a Difference

I designed this chart in the beginning of my career while I was working as a Lifestyle Educator for a hospital-based wellness center. Calculations are averages based on specific brands.

Instead of	Substitute	Fat Calories Saved
1 cup heavy cream	1 cup evaporated skim milk	783
1 cup shredded cheese	1 cup fat free cheese	720
1 cup sour cream	1 cup fat free sour cream	288
1 stick butter	½ cup applesauce ½ cup reduced fat margarine	747 400
½ cup oil	½ cup liquid Butter Buds or ½ cup applesauce or ½ cup plain yogurt	900
1 cup chocolate chips	½ cup chocolate chips	456
1 pound ground beef	1 pound skinless white ground turkey or chicken breast	1,037
2 whole eggs	4 egg whites	94
1 cup mayonnaise	1 cup fat free mayonnaise	1,580
8 ounces cream cheese	8 ounces fat free cream cheese	711

Recipe Modification
Revising a Traditional Recipe

Here are some examples of how you can revise a traditional recipe using the modification techniques of Substitute, Reduce, & Eliminate.

Traditional Recipe	Revised Recipe
Chocolate Cola Cake	
cake mix	cake mix
pudding mix	fat free pudding mix
4 eggs	1 cup fat free Egg Beaters
½ cup oil	½ cup liquid Butter Buds
8 ounces Coke	8 ounces Coke
Corn Dip	
2 cans Mexican-style corn	2 cans Mexican-style corn
1 cup sour cream	1 cup fat free sour cream
1 cup mayonnaise	1 cup fat free mayonnaise
green chilies	green chilies
green onions	green onions
jalapenos	jalapenos
Hello Dollies	
½ cup butter	3 tablespoons reduced fat margarine
	¼ cup liquid Butter Buds
1 cup coconut	¼ cup coconut
	1 cup miniature marshmallows
1 cup chocolate chips	½ cup reduced fat chocolate chips
1 cup pecans	¼ cup pecans
1 can sweetened condensed milk	1 can fat free sweetened condensed milk

Surviving Holidays and Other Celebrations

Did you know that the average American gains 7-10 pounds between Thanksgiving and New Year's Day? Holidays and other special occasions do not have to destroy weight-loss goals. With some advance preparation and a little creativity, anyone can enjoy the all the festivities without feeling guilty or deprived.

It is easy to rationalize our overeating and lack of exercise during the holidays. We say things like, "It's only once a year" or "I'll lose the weight in January." However, as many of us have learned, those pounds often stay with us longer than our New Year's resolutions do! Let's look at some areas in which we might be tempted to let down our guard.

Preparing Christmas "goodies" every year with my mother and grandmother is one of my most special childhood memories. Yet many of those rich treats I remember are loaded with fat and calories. The holiday recipes in this book offer healthier ways to prepare many traditional cookies, cakes, and pies. Sharing holiday baking with your children and grandchildren can teach them about healthy eating.

The holiday dinner can also be prepared to be lower in fat, sodium, or sugar content. Pay attention to portion sizes. Even though the recipes are healthier, servings should still be moderate. Eating slowly and sampling a small portion of several items is one way to watch the calories without feeling deprived. Remember that it takes the body about 20 minutes to feel full. Put a small amount of food on your plate at first and allow yourself to go back for seconds if you are genuinely still hungry. This rule applies to birthday parties, weddings, family reunions, and other gatherings as well.

Many people like to give baked goods as gifts. One way to avoid sampling as you bake is to use my "Christmas in a Jar" recipes, which include only the dry ingredients for cookies, hot chocolate, spiced tea, etc. They are easy to personalize and decorate, and are a thoughtful twist on the traditional baked gift.

Holiday parties are ideal places to socialize—and eat! The combination of delicious food and good conversation makes it easy to consume hundreds of calories without even realizing it. Much of the strategy here is in advance planning. Do not starve yourself before a big event. Instead, eat a healthy snack so that you won't be ravenous when you arrive. I often grab an apple as I leave for a party and eat it on the way.

At the party, determine to socialize away from the food or buffet table. When eating, select foods that are special to the season, instead of ordinary ones you could have anytime at home.

Christmas is the only time of the year that my mother makes her famous Italian cream cheese cake, so I always make plans to balance in a small slice, but I decline to take home any leftovers! Try to find healthier versions of the foods you like. For example, choose white meat without skin, sweet potatoes instead of candied yams, rolls instead of croissants. For dessert, have pumpkin or fruit pie instead of pecan.

The most important strategy for surviving the holidays is changing perspective. If *celebrating* has always meant *eating* to you, try focusing on all the things you have to be thankful for—other than the taste of food. Things like healthy families, freedom, love, and friendships are powerful reminders of the blessings in our lives. They remain long after the food has been eaten and the table has been cleared.

See the chart on the following page for more tips on surviving the holidays.

Tips for Surviving the Holidays and Other Celebrations

Worried about all of the tempting recipes at holiday parties? Prepare a favorite low fat recipe and take it to the event. Not only will you have at least one good choice at the party, but you will also love the feedback as everyone brags about how delicious it is! This and the other tips below can help you "Eat What You Love"— even on special occasions.

- Revise your typical holiday meal to lower the fat content.
- Do not starve yourself before a big event.
- Exercise in the mornings to "start the day off right."
- Continue your exercise routine throughout the holidays.
- Avoid elastic-waist clothing. It will expand with your waistline!
- Make it your goal to maintain your weight during the holidays.
- Plan a non-food reward for reaching your goal.
- Socialize away from the food or buffet table.
- Pay attention to portion sizes.
- Remember that alcoholic beverages and egg nog are very high in calories.
- Curb your appetite with an apple or orange about 30 minutes before a big meal.
- Do away with leftovers.
- Offer low fat snacks when you are entertaining.
- Include more activity during holiday events (take a walk, play a game, etc.)
- Be aware of the things that are stressful for you and may trigger you to overeat.
- Make a list of things other than food for which you are thankful.

What is a Serving?

It is important to learn what a serving is in order to keep calories in balance, especially when trying to lose or control weight. Learning what makes up a serving will make it easier for you to "Eat What You Love" and still meet your goals. How does this approach differ from counting calories? When we simply count calories we are not likely to receive a balance of food intake; therefore, we are probably going to miss out on a lot of essential nutrients. We are all familiar with that awful sluggish feeling that results from either skipping meals or eating the wrong kinds of foods.

I remember counting calories in high school. I'd have a soft drink and a honey bun for breakfast (about 500 calories) and skip lunch. After school, I would grab a candy bar and another soft drink before practice (about 500 calories). For dinner, I'd have everything Mom cooked and more! Balance?

When I was in college, I took a nutrition course and found it very helpful to be able to estimate how many calories I was consuming at any time. Many people still use this system and call it "the diabetic exchange list." The key to using the exchange program is being honest with ourselves about serving sizes. It is easy to tell ourselves that the bowl of cereal we eat for breakfast equals one bread or starch serving, about 80 calories. However in reality most of us eat cereal out of a soup bowl, consuming about three cups which add up to more than 240 calories! I often tell clients that they may need to wear measuring utensils around their waists like a work belt until they measure all the foods they eat and determine how much makes up a serving.

The chart on page 27 titled "What is a Serving?" lists the serving sizes of common foods. Following that are sample five-day meal plans for women and men. Any of my recipes may be used with the meal plans. Simply look at the total calories for one serving and distribute those calories according to the exchanges indicated on the serving chart. For example, one serving of my Chicken and Sausage Gumbo recipe has 330 calories. The calories in that recipe come from meat, rice (or starch), and vegetables. I would count it as two meats (180 calories), one vegetable (25 calories), and one and ½ starch (120 calories).

Don't worry about the calories adding up exactly. You are already doing great by working on the three keys: balance, variety, and moderation. Just measure the food you eat and be honest with yourself about the true sizes of the servings. You'll be more likely to see the results you desire as you "Eat What You Love"!

What is a Serving?

❦ A serving of bread contains about 15 grams carbohydrate, 3 grams protein, a trace of fat, and 80 calories.

❦ A serving of meat or meat substitute contains about 7 grams protein, and 75 calories.

❦ A serving of vegetables contains about 5 grams carbohydrate, 2 grams protein, and 25 calories.

❦ A serving of fruit contains about 15 grams carbohydrate and 60 calories.

❦ A serving of milk or dairy products contains about 12 grams carbohydrate, 8 grams protein and 90 calories.

❦ A serving of fat contains about 5 grams fat and 45 calories.

One Serving of ...	Equals ...
cooked cereal (grits, oatmeal)	½ cup
unsweetened dry cereal	¾ cup
puffed cereal (puffed rice, wheat, etc.)`	1½ cups
cooked white or brown rice	⅓ cup
shredded wheat	½ cup
cooked beans/peas	⅓ cup
baked beans	¼ cup
baked potato	1 small (3 ounces)
bagel	½ bagel
white bread	1 slice
"light" or "diet" bread (40 calories each)	2 slices
fat free popped popcorn	3 cups
pretzels	¾ ounce
lean beef, poultry, fish, pork	1 ounce
tuna canned in water	¼ cup
skim or part skim cheese (i.e. mozzarella)	1 ounce
cooked green beans, carrots, spinach	½ cup
raw broccoli, cauliflower, carrots, spinach	1 cup
apple	1 small (4 ounces)
banana	½ banana
cantaloupe	⅓ melon (3 ounces)
fruit cocktail, applesauce	½ cup
grapefruit	½ melon
grapes	15 grapes
canned peaches	½ cup
skim milk	1 cup
nonfat yogurt	8 ounces

Sample Daily Menu for Weight Loss #1

(Women—1200 calories/day)

Remember that this is an example of a typical day. Do not eat the same foods every day. Variety is the key to staying on track!

Breakfast:

1 BREAD	2 slices light bread/toast
1 MILK	2 slices fat free cheese
1 MILK	1 cup skim milk

Snack:

1 FRUIT	1 apple or fruit serving of your choice

Lunch:

1 BREAD	2 slices light bread
1 MEAT	2 slices 98% fat free lunch meat (ham/turkey; not to exceed 75 calories)
1½ BREAD	baked chips/pretzels (not to exceed 120 calories)
1 FRUIT	fruit serving of your choice

Snack:

1 VEGETABLE	1 cup raw vegetables
FREE	2 tablespoons fat free dressing
FREE	sugar free beverage

Dinner:

3 MEAT	3 ounces baked meat (lean beef/chicken)
1½ BREAD	¾ cup mashed potatoes with fat free gravy
2 VEGETABLES	½ cup cooked squash
	½ cup cooked green beans
	(or 1 cup vegetable of your choice)

Sample Daily Menu for Weight Loss #1

(Men—1500 calories/day)

Remember that this is an example of a typical day. Do not eat the same foods every day. Variety is the key to staying on track!

Breakfast:

1 BREAD	2 slices light bread/toast
1 MILK	2 slices fat free cheese
1 MILK	1 cup skim milk

Snack:

1 FRUIT	1 apple or fruit serving of your choice

Lunch:

2 BREAD	4 slices light bread
2 MEAT	4 slices 98% fat free lunch meat (ham/turkey; not to exceed 75 calories)
1½ BREAD	baked chips/pretzels (not to exceed 120 calories)
1 FRUIT	fruit serving of your choice

Snack:

1 VEGETABLE	1 cup raw vegetables
FREE	2 tablespoons fat free dressing
FREE	sugar free beverage

Dinner:

4 MEAT	4 ounces baked meat (lean beef/chicken)
1½ BREAD	¾ cup mashed potatoes with fat free gravy
2 VEGETABLE	½ cup cooked squash
	½ cup cooked green beans
	(or 1 cup vegetable of your choice)
1 BREAD	1 small roll

Sample Daily Menu for Weight Loss #2

(Women—1200 calories/day)

Balance in that favorite dinner by saving the needed servings. Example if you want pasta for dinner have fewer bread or starch servings at lunch.

Breakfast:

1½ BREAD	McDonald's plain biscuit
1 FAT	
1 FRUIT	½ cup orange juice
FREE	1 jelly

Snack:

1 FRUIT	1 apple or fruit serving of your choice

Lunch:

1 BREAD	2 slices light (diet) bread
2 MEAT	½ cup canned tuna or chicken canned in water
1 FAT	2 teaspoons diet/light mayonnaise
1 BREAD	baked chips or pretzels (not to exceed 80 calories)
1 VEGETABLE	1 cup raw vegetables of your choice
FREE	2-3 tablespoons fat free dressing

Snack: *Special*

2 MILK	fat free ice cream or yogurt (not to exceed 180 calories)
1 FRUIT	fruit topping (no syrup)
FREE	sugar free beverage

Dinner:

2 MEAT	1 serving Low Fat Cheesy Chicken & Spaghetti (page 151)
1½ BREAD	
2 VEGETABLE	1 cup cooked vegetable of your choice (i.e. green beans)

Sample Daily Menu for Weight Loss #2

(Men—1500 calories/day)

Balance in that favorite dinner by saving the needed servings. Example if you want pasta for dinner have fewer bread or starch servings at lunch.

Breakfast:
1½ BREAD   McDonald's plain biscuit
1 FAT
1 MEAT   1 slice Canadian bacon
1 FRUIT   ½ cup orange juice
FREE   1 jelly

Snack:
1 FRUIT   1 apple or fruit serving of your choice

Lunch:
2 BREAD   4 slices light (diet) bread
3 MEAT   ¾ cup canned tuna or chicken in water
1 FAT   2 teaspoons light (diet) mayonnaise
1 BREAD   baked chips or pretzels
                (not to exceed 80 calories)
1 VEGETABLE 1 cup raw vegetables of your choice
FREE   2-3 tablespoons fat free dressing

Snack: *Special*
2 MILK   fat free ice cream or yogurt
                (not to exceed 180 calories)
1 FRUIT   fruit topping (no syrup)
FREE   sugar free beverage

Dinner:
2 MEAT   1 serving Low Fat Cheesy Chicken &
                Spaghetti (page 151)
1½ BREAD
2 VEGETABLE 1 cup cooked vegetable of your choice
                (i.e. green beans)
1 BREAD   1 roll

Sample Daily Menu for Weight Loss #3

(Women—1200 Calories)

When dining out, select a lean cut of meat or grilled fish/shrimp without butter/ sauces. You may have to skip the bread. If you go to the salad bar keep it simple! Choose salad greens and vegetables; avoid meats, cheeses, and eggs.

Breakfast:

2 BREAD	1½ cup dry cereal
1 MILK	1 cup skim milk
1 FRUIT	½ banana

Snack:

1 MILK	8 ounces low fat yogurt
1 FRUIT	½ banana

Lunch: *Chef Salad*

2 BREAD	8 crackers
1 MEAT	1 ounce lean ham
1 VEGETABLE	1 cup raw vegetables of your choice
1 FAT	4 tablespoons light salad dressing
OR	
FREE	2-3 tablespoons fat free dressing

Snack:

1 FRUIT	1 orange
FREE	sugar free beverage

Dinner: *Dining Out*

3 MEAT	3 ounces broiled lean beef (Filet Mignon)
1 BREAD	small baked potato
1 VEG.	½ cup cooked vegetable of your choice
FREE	large green salad

Sample Daily Menu for Weight Loss #3

(Men—1500 calories/day)

When dining out, select a lean cut of meat or grilled fish/shrimp without butter/ sauces. You may have to skip the bread. If you go to the salad bar keep it simple! Choose salad greens and vegetables; avoid meats, cheeses, and eggs.

Breakfast:

2 BREAD	1½ cup dry cereal
1 MILK	1 cup skim milk
1 FRUIT	½ banana

Snack:

1 MILK	8 ounces low fat yogurt
1 FRUIT	½ banana

Lunch: *Chef Salad*

3 BREAD	12 crackers
2 MEAT	2 ounces lean ham
1 VEGETABLE	1 cup raw vegetables of your choice
1 FAT	4 tablespoons light salad dressing
OR	
FREE	2-3 tablespoons fat free dressing

Snack:

1 FRUIT	1 orange
FREE	sugar free beverage

Dinner: *Dining Out*

4 MEAT	4 ounces broiled lean beef (Filet Mignon)
1 BREAD	small baked potato
1 VEG.	½ cup cooked vegetable of your choice
1 BREAD	1 small roll/toast (without butter)
FREE	large green salad

Sample Daily Menu for Weight Loss #4

(Women—1200 calories/day)

When cooking vegetables, I season with 98% fat free ham lunch meat and 1-2 tablespoons reduced fat/calorie margarine. If selecting vegetables in a restaurant, be aware that added fat that may be present during the cooking process.

Breakfast:

1 BREAD	½ cup cooked cereal (grits or oatmeal)
1 BREAD	2 slices light (diet) bread toast
1 FRUIT	½ cup orange juice
1 FAT	1 strip bacon

Snack:

1 MILK	8 ounces low fat yogurt
1 FRUIT	½ cup mixed fruit

Lunch:

1 BREAD	½ cup black eye peas
1 BREAD	1 small piece cornbread (2 × 2 inches)
3 MEAT	3 ounces baked meat
2 VEGETABLE	1 cup cooked vegetables of your choice (i.e. ½ cup cabbage and ½ cup turnip greens)
1 FAT	added during cooking

Snack:

1 FRUIT	1 orange
FREE	sugar free beverage

Dinner:

1 MEAT	1 serving **Low Fat Taco Soup** (page 79)
1 BREAD	
FREE	large green salad

Sample Daily Menu for Weight Loss #4

(Men—1500 calories/day)

When cooking vegetables, I season with 98% fat free ham lunch meat and 1-2 tablespoons reduced fat/calorie margarine. If selecting vegetables in a restaurant, be aware that added fat that may be present during the cooking process.

Breakfast:

2 BREAD	1 cup cooked cereal (grits or oatmeal)
1 BREAD	2 slices light (diet) bread toast
1 FRUIT	½ cup orange juice
1 FAT	1 strip bacon

Snack:

1 MILK	8 ounces low fat yogurt
1 FRUIT	½ cup mixed fruit

Lunch:

1 BREAD	½ cup black eye peas
1 BREAD	1 small piece cornbread (2 × 2 inches)
4 MEAT	4 ounces baked meat
2 VEG.	1 cup cooked vegetables of your choice (i.e. ½ cup cabbage and ½ cup turnip greens)
1 FAT	added during cooking

Snack:

1 FRUIT	1 orange
FREE	sugar free beverage

Dinner:

2 MEAT	2 servings **Low Fat Taco Soup** (page 79)
2 BREAD	
FREE	large green salad

Sample Daily Menu for Weight Loss #5

(Women—1200 calories/day)

After dining out at lunch, you may find that you have few food choices left at dinner if you are to stay within your calorie plan for the day. This may be a good time to use a frozen dinner that does not have meat exchanges, or a large baked potato (2 breads), 2 slices fat free cheese (1 milk) and a green salad (free).

Breakfast:

1 BREAD	2 slices light (diet) bread
1 MILK	2 slices fat free/low fat cheese (no more than 45 calories/slice)

Snack:

1 FRUIT	1 cup fresh mixed fruit
FREE	sugar free gelatin
FREE	fat free Cool Whip

Lunch: *Dining Out*

1 BREAD	½ large or 1 small baked potato
1 BREAD	1 hush puppy
3 MEAT	½ dozen grilled shrimp

Salad Bar

1 VEGETABLE	½ cup raw vegetables of your choice
FREE	salad greens/lettuce
1 MEAT	1 tablespoon cheese and 1 tablespoon ham or egg
1 FAT	2-3 tablespoons reduced calorie salad dressing

Snack:

1 FRUIT	fruit serving of your choice
FREE	sugar free beverage

Dinner:

2 BREAD	1½ cup dry cereal
1 MILK	1 cup skim milk
1 FRUIT	½ banana

Sample Daily Menu for Weight Loss #5

(Men—1500 calories/day)

After dining out at lunch, you may find that you have few food choices left at dinner if you are to stay within your calorie plan for the day. This may be a good time to use a frozen dinner that does not have meat exchanges, or a large baked potato (2 breads), 2 slices fat free cheese (1 milk) and a green salad (free).

Breakfast:

2 MEAT	2 slices Canadian bacon
1 BREAD	2 slices light (diet) bread
1 MILK	2 slices fat free/low fat cheese
	(no more than 45 calories/slice)

Snack:

1 FRUIT	1 cup fresh mixed fruit
FREE	sugar free gelatin
FREE	fat free Cool Whip

Lunch: *Dining Out*

1 BREAD	½ large or 1 small baked potato
1 BREAD	1 hush puppy
3 MEAT	½ dozen grilled shrimp

Salad Bar

1 VEGETABLE	½ cup raw vegetables of your choice
FREE	salad greens/lettuce
1 MEAT	1 tablespoon cheese and 1 tablespoon
	ham or egg
1 FAT	2-3 tablespoons reduced calorie salad dressing

Snack:

1 FRUIT	fruit serving of your choice
FREE	sugar free beverage

Dinner:

3 BREAD	2¼ cups dry cereal
1 MILK	1 cup skim milk
1 FRUIT	½ banana

"Variety is the key. If you eat the same things you'll get bored. So, make some changes & have fun. Focus on being healthy & happy with yourself, not just numbers on a scale."

APPETIZERS *&* BEVERAGES

"Let the Good Times Roll!"

Fat Free
Chicken Enchilada Dip

1   pound fat free cream
    cheese, softened
1½ cups shredded fat
    free cheddar cheese
2   (10-ounce) cans
    98% fat free
    white chicken

1   teaspoon minced
    garlic
1   (10-ounce) can
    extra hot Rotel
    tomatoes, drained
    fresh cilantro, chopped
    green onions, chopped

Stir cream cheese and shredded cheese together until well blended. Add the chicken, garlic, tomatoes, cilantro, and green onions and mix well. Cover and chill until serving. Serve with fat free baked tortilla chips or crackers.

Yield: 22 servings of ¼ cup each
❦ *Calories: 65*
❦ *Fat: less than 1 gram*

Fat Free Corn Dip

2 (11-ounce) cans Mexican-style corn, drained
1 cup fat free sour cream
1 cup fat free mayonnaise
1 small can green chilies
jalapeno peppers to taste, finely chopped
2-3 green onions, chopped
1 cup shredded fat free cheddar cheese

Combine corn, sour cream, and mayonnaise. Add chilies, jalapeno peppers and onions to mixture; stir in cheese. Chill before serving.

Yield: 25 servings of ¼ cup each
❦ *Calories: 40*
❦ *Fat: 0 grams*

Fat Free Spectacular Spinach Dip

Serve this party favorite with fresh vegetables and reduced fat crackers.

1   container fat free French onion dip (prepared)
4   ounces fat free cream cheese
9   ounces frozen spinach, thawed and drained
¼   cup celery, chopped
2   green onions, sliced
3   tablespoons pimientos, diced
⅓   cup water chestnuts, chopped
½   teaspoon garlic powder
2   tablespoons fat free creamy Italian salad dressing mix

In a medium bowl, combine French onion dip and cream cheese; beat with wire whisk until smooth. Add spinach and remaining ingredients; mix well. Cover and refrigerate until serving.

Yield: 32 servings of 1 tablespoon each
❦ *Calories: 20*
❦ *Fat: 0 grams*

Low Fat Creamy Artichoke and Broccoli Dip

Serve this dip warm with your favorite low fat chips or crackers.

1	onion, chopped	Tabasco Pepper Sauce to taste
1	tablespoon minced garlic	⅛ teaspoon pepper
2	tablespoons reduced fat margarine	⅛ teaspoon Lawry's Seasoned Salt
1	(10-ounce) package frozen broccoli, thawed	½ cup low fat mayonnaise
1	(13¾-ounce) can artichoke hearts, drained and chopped	12 ounces fat free cream cheese
8	ounces reduced fat Velveeta cheese, cut up	½ cup freshly grated Parmesan cheese
1	teaspoon Worcester-shire sauce	juice of one lemon
		paprika and parsley to garnish

Preheat oven to 350°. Sauté the onion and garlic in a skillet with melted margarine. Add broccoli, artichoke hearts, and Velveeta. Sauté over low heat until blended. Add seasonings. In a mixing bowl, cream mayonnaise, cream cheese, and Parmesan cheese with lemon juice. Add broccoli mixture to cream cheese mixture. Spoon into 8 × 8-inch baking pan. Bake at 350° for 25 minutes or simmer in slow cooker. Garnish with paprika and parsley before serving.

Yield: 20 servings of ¼ cup each
❦ *Calories: 80*   ❦ *Fat: 2½ grams*

Low Fat Dip Chips

8 corn tortillas   chili powder
cumin seasoning   garlic salt or powder

Using a sharp knife, cut tortilla stack into 8 wedges. Spread wedges on a nonstick cookie sheet. Spray top of tortilla wedges with nonstick cooking spray. Sprinkle with seasonings to taste. Bake at 400° for 10 minutes or until crisp, turning once. Do not overbake. Let cool for about 5 minutes before serving. Store leftover chips in an airtight container. Before serving, freshen chips in microwave for about 45 seconds.

Yield: About 2 servings of 20 chips each
❦ *Calories: 100*
❦ *Fat: 1 gram*

Low Fat Seven-Layer Tex Mex Dip

1 (16-ounce) can fat
  free refried beans
1 cup salsa
1 cup fat free
  sour cream plus
  1½ tablespoons
  taco seasoning
1 small container
  avocado dip
2 tablespoons
  chopped ripe olives

1 cup (4 ounces)
  shredded reduced
  fat cheddar or
  Monterey Jack
  cheese
2 medium tomatoes,
  chopped
¼ cup sliced green
  onions

In a medium bowl, stir together the refried beans and salsa. Spread the bean mixture into a 9-inch platter or pie plate. Spread the sour cream on top of the bean layer. Spread avocado dip on the sour cream. Layer the shredded cheese, tomatoes, green onions and olives on top. If desired, cover and refrigerate for up to 4 hours. Serve with reduced fat tortilla chips.

Yield: 16 servings
❦ *Calories: 80*
❦ *Fat: 3 grams*

Reduced Fat Cheesy Chili Dip

Perfect for Super Bowl parties!

1   pound reduced fat Velveeta cheese, cut up

1   (15-ounce) can turkey chili

1   (10-ounce) can diced Rotel tomatoes

Sour cream for garnish, if desired

Microwave Velveeta, chili, and Rotel tomatoes on high setting for five minutes or until melted. For garnish, cut a small hole in a plastic bag and fill with sour cream. Squeeze garnish over dip to make "football laces."

Yield: 15 servings of ¼ cup each
☙ *Calories: 93*
☙ *Fat: 3.6 grams*

Reduced Fat
Cheesy Crawfish Dip

Try serving this recipe over rice or pasta.
Just add liquid (i.e. chicken broth)
to desired consistency.

2 tablespoons reduced fat margarine
½ cup chopped onion
½ cup chopped bell pepper
½ cup chopped celery
1 bunch green onions, chopped
1-2 tablespoons minced garlic
1 pound peeled crawfish tails, chopped
1 pound reduced fat Velveeta cheese, cubed
1 (10-ounce) can reduced fat cream of mushroom soup
1 (10-ounce) can cream of shrimp soup
red pepper to taste

Melt margarine in skillet; add vegetables and minced garlic. Sauté over low heat until soft; add crawfish and heat 15-20 minutes or until crawfish are cooked. Add cubed cheese, soups, and red pepper; heat until well blended. Serve hot with low fat chips or crackers.

Yield: 24 servings
🦐 *Calories: 80*
🦐 *Fat: 3 grams*

Reduced Fat Hot Seafood Dip

1 (8-ounces) package light cream cheese

⅓ cup reduced fat margarine

1 tablespoon Worcestershire sauce

1 teaspoon garlic powder

chives to taste

parsley to taste

1 (6-ounce) can crab meat

1 (6-ounce) can tiny shrimp or crawfish tails

Tabasco Pepper Sauce to taste

Soften cream cheese and butter in microwave and stir until smooth. Add Worcestershire sauce, garlic salt, chives, and parsley; stir. Add crab and shrimp; stir. Keep warm in slow cooker or chafing dish.

Yield: 24 servings
❦ Calories: 45 (using canned shrimp)
❦ Fat: 3 grams

Reduced Fat Cajun Shrimp Dip

¼ cup fat free liquid Butter Buds
¼ cup fat free chicken broth
½ cup flour
1 medium bell pepper, finely chopped
3 large stalks celery, finely chopped
1 (10¾-ounce) can reduced fat cream of mushroom soup
1 pound small shrimp, peeled
salt, pepper, cayenne pepper, and paprika to taste

Blend liquid Butter Buds, broth and flour in large saucepan. Add vegetables and sauté over medium heat until tender, about 20-30 minutes. Add soup and mix well. Add shrimp while continually stirring; cook shrimp until they turn pink. Season to taste. For best results, reduce heat and allow dip to simmer in covered saucepan or slow cooker until shrimp are tender.

Yield: 25 servings of 2 tablespoons each
❦ *Calories: 28*
❦ *Fat: .6 gram*

Christmas in a Jar
Mexican Dip Mix

½ cup dried parsley   ⅓ cup chili powder
⅓ cup minced onion   ¼ cup ground cumin
¼ cup dried chives   ¼ cup salt

In a large bowl, combine spices and pour into an airtight container. To present as a gift, attach a card that reads:

"Mexican Dip Mix"

Combine 3 tablespoons dip mix with 1 cup light mayonnaise and 1 cup fat free sour cream. Yield 32 servings of 1 tablespoon each.

Yield: 32 servings
❦ *Calories: 25*
❦ *Fat: less than 1 gram*

Catfish Party Dip

2 catfish fillets, baked or steamed
1 cup low fat sour cream
4 ounces fat free cream cheese
1 tablespoon pickle relish
½ teaspoon paprika
3 tablespoons "Made in Louisiana" hot sauce (use less for milder taste)

Mix all ingredients well with a blender, food processor, or wire whisk. Serve with chips, crackers or vegetables.

Yield: 16 servings
❦ *Calories: 50*
❦ *Fat: 2 grams*

Fat Free
Easy Shrimp Dip

½ pound boiled
   seasoned shrimp
6 ounces fat free cream
   cheese, softened
¼ cup fat free
   mayonnaise

½ bunch green
   onions, tops only
½ -1 stalk celery
red pepper
paprika
salt and pepper

Peel shrimp and chop in food processor. Blend softened cream cheese with shrimp; add mayonnaise. Chop green onion tops and celery very fine; add to shrimp mixture. Season to taste. Chill at least 4-6 hours until flavors are well blended.

Yield: 24 servings
❦ *Calories: 15*
❦ *Fat: 0 grams*

Nantucket Crab

4 ounces fat free cream cheese	¾ cup chili sauce
½ cup low fat mayonnaise	1 cup lump crab meat
	2 tablespoons chopped parsley

Mix cream cheese and mayonnaise. Spread in the bottom of a 6 × 8-inch serving dish. Cover mixture with chili sauce. Place crab meat on top and sprinkle with parsley. Chill and serve with reduced fat thin wheat crackers.

Yield: 6 servings
❦ *Calories: 80*
❦ *Fat: ½ gram*

Low Fat Ham Roll Ups

8 ounces fat free cream cheese	1 (10-ounce) package 98% fat free ham (rectangle slices)
¼ cup crushed pineapple, drained	

Mix cream cheese with pineapple. Spread mixture on ham slices and roll ham. Slice into bite sized pieces. Place toothpick in each piece.

Yield: About 30 servings
❦ *Calories: 18*
❦ *Fat: .3 grams*

Low Fat Spicy Chicken Quesadillas

4   boneless skinless chicken breasts, cooked and shredded
1   (1¼-ounce) package taco seasoning
1   can Rotel tomatoes, chopped and drained
5   tablespoons shredded Mexican cheese blend
10 fat free flour tortillas
5   teaspoons reduced fat margarine

Combine cooked chicken with taco seasoning and toss. Heat chicken over high to medium heat in large nonstick skillet. Remove chicken and set aside. Spread ½ teaspoon margarine on a tortilla and place in skillet. Add Rotel tomatoes, 1 tablespoon cheese, and chicken. Place another tortilla, which has also been spread with ½ teaspoon margarine, on top. Cook until mixture is melted. Repeat with remaining tortillas. Cut each quesadilla into 4 pieces and serve warm.

Yield: 20 appetizers
❦ *Calories: 63*
❦ *Fat: 1.5 grams*

Fat Free Tortilla Roll Ups

8 ounces fat free cream cheese
½ pint fat free sour cream
1 teaspoon garlic powder
1 small can chili peppers
8 fat free flour tortillas
1 (12-ounce) jar salsa

Combine all ingredients except salsa. Spread mixture thinly on tortillas. Roll tortillas and refrigerate for one hour. Slice into small bite-sized pieces and insert toothpick in each piece. Dip in salsa.

Yield: About 40 servings
❦ *Calories: 30*
❦ *Fat: 0 grams*

Low Fat Ham Delights

You may prepare these mini sandwiches
in advance and freeze them.
Add about 10 minutes to baking time.

1 cup reduced fat margarine
3 tablespoons mustard
1 tablespoon poppy seed
1 medium onion, grated and drained on paper towel (optional)

1 teaspoon Worcestershire sauce
fat free Swiss cheese slices
1 pound boiled ham, shaved
2 (8-count) packages small, pre-baked rolls or buns

Mix together margarine, mustard, poppy seed, onion, and Worcestershire. Without separating rolls, slice bread in half lengthwise and spread bottom half with a thick layer of margarine mixture. Add cheese and ham and cover with top layer of rolls. Return rolls to foil pan. Cut rolls individually and wrap each roll tightly with aluminum foil. Bake at 400° for about 15 minutes or until cheese melts. Serving size is 1 roll or bun, 2 slices fat free cheese, 3 slices shaved ham and 2 tablespoons margarine mixture.

Yield: 16 servings
❦ *Calories: 240*
❦ *Fat: 8 grams*

Fat Free Nibblers

3 cups oven toasted corn square cereal
3 cups oven toasted rice square cereal
1 cup Cheerios
2 cups fat free pretzel sticks
4 tablespoons liquid Butter Buds
4-5 dashes Tabasco Pepper Sauce
1 tablespoon lemon juice
2 tablespoons Worcestershire sauce
1 teaspoon garlic powder
1 teaspoon onion powder
1 teaspoon Italian seasoning
1½ teaspoons taco seasoning
½ teaspoon oregano
2 teaspoons Tony Chachere's Original Seasoning

Pour cereal, Cheerios, and pretzels into a gallon-size plastic zip bag. In a skillet over low heat, combine Butter Buds, Tabasco, lemon juice, Worcestershire sauce, and seasonings. Pour seasoning mixture into bag and shake well. Prepare cookie sheet with nonstick cooking spray and spread mixture onto cookie sheet. Bake at 250° for about 45 minutes, stirring every 15 minutes. Sprinkle with additional Tony Chachere's seasoning during baking, if desired.

Yield: 18 servings of ½ cup each
❦ *Calories: 60*
❦ *Fat: 0 grams*

Low Fat Veggie Bars

Ideal for parties!

1 can reduced fat crescent dinner rolls	1 bunch green onions, finely chopped
8 ounces fat free cream cheese	1 cup broccoli, finely chopped
½ package ranch style dressing mix	1-2 tomatoes, finely chopped
4 tablespoons reduced fat mayonnaise	½ cup shredded fat free cheddar cheese

Spray a 9 × 13-inch cookie sheet with nonstick cooking spray. Without separating, unroll can of crescent rolls and shape to fit cookie sheet. Bake rolls at 350° for 15 minutes until golden in color. Mix cream cheese, dressing mix and mayonnaise. Spread over cooled crust to edges. Sprinkle green onions over cream cheese mixture. Add broccoli and tomatoes, pressing vegetables lightly into cream cheese mixture. Sprinkle with cheddar cheese and press. Cover cookie sheet tightly with plastic wrap and chill. When ready to serve, cut into bars. Bars will remain fresh for about 48 hours if chilled and well sealed.

Yield: 48 small bars
❦ Calories: 30
❦ Fat: 1 gram

Yogurt Fruit Dressing

¼ cup granulated
   sugar
8 teaspoons cornstarch
2 cups pineapple juice

½ cup lemon juice
½ cup orange juice
1 cup plain nonfat
   yogurt

Combine sugar, cornstarch, and juices in double boiler and cook until thickened, stirring constantly. Allow to cool. Fold in yogurt. Serve with fresh fruit.

Yield: 15 servings of 2 tablespoons each
❦ *Calories: 30*
❦ *Fat: 0 grams*

Fat Free
Crabmeat Surprise Tray

8   ounces fat free
    cream cheese
1½ cups ketchup
2   tablespoons
    horseradish
1   tablespoon lemon
    juice
2½ teaspoons Worcester-
    shire sauce

salt and pepper to taste
½   pound fat free
    crabmeat (Louis
    Kemp Seafood,
    Crab Delights)
fresh parsley to
    garnish
crackers (any variety)

Spread cream cheese on shallow platter. Prepare red sauce by combining ketchup, horseradish sauce, lemon juice, and Worcestershire sauce in a separate bowl. Season to taste with salt and pepper. Spread red sauce in center of cream cheese. Sprinkle crabmeat on top of red sauce and garnish with parsley. Place crackers around outer edge.

Yield: 12 servings
❧ *Calories: 70 (without crackers)*
❧ *Fat: 0*

Low Fat
Ham & Cheese Biscuits

3 cups low fat biscuit and baking mix

1 cup reduced fat ham, finely chopped

1 cup reduced fat shredded cheddar cheese

1 cup fat free shredded cheddar cheese

¼ cup fat free Parmesan cheese

2 tablespoons parsley flakes

2 teaspoons prepared spicy mustard

²/₃ cup skim milk

2 tablespoons reduced fat margarine, melted

Preheat oven to 350°. Spray baking sheet with nonstick cooking spray. Combine all ingredients except melted margarine and mix well. Shape mixture into 1-inch balls. Place on baking sheet and bake 20-25 minutes or until brown. Brush tops of biscuits with melted margarine. Remove immediately from baking sheet and serve warm.

Yield: 6 dozen small appetizers
❦ *Calories: 40*
❦ *Fat: ½ gram*

Bugs on a Log

1	banana	1	tablespoon raisins
1	tablespoon reduced fat peanut butter		

Spread peanut butter over banana. Sprinkle with raisins.

Yield: 1 serving
❦ *Calories: 270*
❦ *Fat: 5½ grams*

Peanut Butter Squares

6	fat free saltine crackers	¼	cup miniature marshmallows
1	tablespoon reduced fat peanut butter		

Spread peanut butter thinly over each cracker. Top with miniature marshmallows. Bake at 375° for about 5 minutes until marshmallows are toasted brown.

Yield: 1 serving
❦ *Calories: 200*
❦ *Fat: 5½ grams*

Pizza Squares

8 reduced fat Triscuit crackers	¼ cup pizza sauce (in squeeze bottle)
¼ cup shredded fat free cheddar cheese	

Arrange crackers on a microwave-safe plate. Squeeze each cracker with pizza sauce and top with cheese. Microwave for 30-45 seconds or until cheese melts.

Yield: 1 serving
❦ *Calories: 215*
❦ *Fat: 4½ grams*

Fat Free Wassil

This is also an excellent "Christmas in a Jar" gift!

1 gallon apple cider	1 cup lemon juice
1 quart orange juice	4 sticks cinnamon
1 quart pineapple juice	24 cloves

In large saucepan, combine all ingredients and stir over low to medium heat until well blended. Let cool. Stores well in refrigerator for 2-3 weeks. Reheat at serving.

Yield: 25 servings of 1 cup each
❦ *Calories: 130*
❦ *Fat: 0*

Red Hot Punch

*This festive punch is ideal for Christmas parties,
or pour into jars and give as gifts!
Decorate jars with cinnamon sticks and ribbon.*

1   quart apple juice
2   sticks cinnamon
6   cloves or ¼ teaspoon

3½ ounces Red Hots
    candies

Combine ingredients and heat to dissolve; serve hot.

Yield: 8 servings
❦ *Calories: 100*
❦ *Fat: 0 grams*

Christmas in a Jar
Sugar Free Spiced Tea

½ cup lemon flavored
  instant tea

2 cups sugar free
  instant orange drink

2 cups sugar
  substitute

2 teaspoons
  cinnamon

1 teaspoon ground
  cloves

Combine ingredients in large bowl. Pour into a 1-quart wide-mouthed glass jar. Place lid on top. Cut an 8-inch circle of fabric to cover lid. Place fabric over lid; secure in place with ribbon or raffia. Decorate as desired.

Attach a card that reads:

"Sugar Free Spiced Tea"

Fill cup with 1 tablespoon mix and add 1 cup hot water.

Yield: 40
❦ *Calories: 50*
❦ *Fat: 0*

Christmas in a Jar Hot Chocolate Mix

Christmas in a Jar recipes make great gifts, and since you aren't actually baking anything, you won't be tempted to sample!

1 (1-pound) box instant hot chocolate mix	½ box powdered sugar
1 (6-ounce) jar lite coffee creamer	1 (4-quart) box powdered milk

Combine ingredients in large bowl. Pour into a 1-quart wide-mouth glass jar. Place lid on top. Cut an 8-inch circle of fabric to cover lid. Place fabric over lid; secure in place with ribbon or raffia. Decorate as desired.

Attach a card that reads:

"Hot Chocolate Mix"

Fill cup with 5 tablespoons mix and finish filling cup with hot water.

Yield: 40 servings
❦ Calories: 160
❦ Fat: 0

Sugar Free Punch

2 (.35-ounce) packages sugar free Kool Aid fruit punch
1 large (46-ounce) can pineapple juice

2 quarts water
1 (2-liter) Diet Sprite or 7-up

Mix all ingredients and chill before serving.

Yield: 24 servings of about 1 cup each
❦ *Calories: 30*

Strawberry Yogurt Smoothie

*Add fat free ice cream to make a great
fat free yogurt sundae!*

1 cup strawberries with stems removed	1 tablespoon honey
½ cup plain yogurt	2 ice cubes
1 cup orange juice	low fat granola (optional)
	honey (optional)

Combine all ingredients in blender and blend until smooth. Top with low fat granola and honey.

Yield: 2 servings
❦ *Calories: 140 (without topping)*
❦ *Fat: 0 grams*

Almond Tea

*Serve this refreshing tea with an ice ring, cherries,
and slices of lemon, orange, and lime.*

1½ quarts water
1¼ cups granulated
    sugar
juice of one lemon
grated lemon peel
1 (6-ounce) can
    frozen lemonade
    concentrate

2 cups strong tea
    (1 family tea bag
    plus 2 cups water)
1 tablespoon vanilla
    extract
1 tablespoon almond
    extract

Combine water and sugar in saucepan and stir until
dissolved. Add lemon juice, peel, and frozen
concentrate. Simmer 3-5 minutes. Add tea and bring
to a boil. Remove and stir in extracts.

Yield: 16 servings
❦ *Calories: 85*
❦ *Fat: 0 grams*

"When our lives are balanced, we have a sense of

control. When we're in control, we have a feeling of

accomplishment & we can be happy with ourselves."

SOUPS
SALADS
BREADS
VEGETABLES

"Put It All Together"

Southwest Vegetable Soup

1 (10¾-ounce) can zesty tomato soup or sauce
1 (10½-ounce) can chicken broth
3 cups water
1 (15¼-ounce) can whole kernel corn, drained
1 (14½-ounce) can cut green beans, drained
1 (14½-ounce) can Mexican-style stewed tomatoes, undrained
1 (4-ounce) can chopped green chilies, drained
1 package taco seasoning
8 round corn tortillas, cut into ½-inch strips
½ cup shredded reduced fat Monterey Jack cheese

Combine soup, broth, water, corn, green beans, tomatoes, chilies, and seasoning in a Dutch oven. Bring to a boil over medium-high heat. Reduce heat and simmer for about 10 minutes. Slowly stir in tortilla strips and cheese. Continue to cook until tortilla strips are softened and cheese is melted.

Yield: 10 servings
❧ *Calories: 170*
❧ *Fat: 5 grams*

Reduced Fat Wild Rice Soup

2 tablespoons margarine
2 medium stalks celery, sliced (about 1 cup)
1 medium carrot, coarsely grated (about 1 cup)
1 medium onion, chopped (about ½ cup)
1 small green bell pepper, chopped (about ½ cup)
3 tablespoons all-purpose flour
¼ teaspoon pepper
1½ cups cooked wildrice
1 cup water
1 (10¾-ounce) can condensed chicken broth
1 cup evaporated milk
⅓ cup slivered almonds, toasted
¼ cup chopped fresh parsley

Heat margarine in 3-quart saucepan over medium heat. Cook celery, carrot, onion, and bell pepper in margarine about 4 minutes. Stir in flour and pepper. Stir in wild rice, water, and chicken broth. Heat to boiling; reduce heat, cover and simmer 15 minutes (or less for crisper vegetables). Stir occasionally. Stir in milk, almonds, and parsley. Heat just until hot. Do not boil.

Yield: 8 servings
❦ *Calories: 155*
❦ *Fat: 5½ grams*

Christmas in a Jar
Nine Bean Soup Mix

1 pound barley pearls
1 pound dried black beans
1 pound dried red beans
1 pound dried pinto beans
1 pound dried navy beans

1 pound dried Great Northern beans
1 pound dried lentils
1 pound dried split peas
1 pound dried black-eyed peas

Seasoning (Add to each 2-cup portion):

1 tablespoon minced onion
1 teaspoon minced garlic

¾ teaspoon salt
¾ teaspoon black pepper

Combine all beans. Divide into ten 2-cup portions for gift giving, and pour into jars or gift packages. Add all seasonings to each package, and attach a gift card with the following recipe:

(Continued on next page.)

(Continued from page 74.)

"Nine Bean Soup"

2 cups Nine Bean Soup mix
2 quarts water
6 slices 98% fat free ham

1 (16-ounce) can tomatoes, undrained and chopped
1 (10-ounce) can tomatoes and green chilies, undrained

Sort and wash 2 cups bean mix; place in a Dutch oven. Cover with water 2 inches above beans, and soak overnight. Drain beans; add 2 quarts water and ham. Cover and bring to a boil; reduce heat and simmer 1½ hours or until beans are tender. Add remaining ingredients and simmer 30 minutes, stirring occasionally.

Yield: 8 servings of 1 cup each
❦ *Calories: 125*
❦ *Fat: 0 grams*

Reduced Fat Taco Soup

This recipe is great cooked in a slow cooker
on low temperature for 4 or more hours.
The longer the flavors have to blend, the better!
Garnish with shredded cheese, reduced fat
sour cream, and chopped green onions.
Serve with baked tortilla chips.

1	pound lean ground beef	1	can ranch style beans
1	onion, chopped	1	can diced tomatoes
1	package Ranch dressing mix	1	can pinto beans
1	package taco seasoning	1	can Mexican-style corn
1	can Mexican-style Rotel tomatoes	1	can white shoepeg corn
1	can chopped chilies	1	can white hominy
		3	cups water

Brown ground beef and onion; add taco seasoning mix and dressing mix. In a large boiler or slow cooker, combine all ingredients. Use liquid in all vegetables; do not drain. Cook until heated thoroughly.

Yield: 18 servings of 1 cup each
❦ *Calories: 170*
❦ *Fat: 3 grams*

Reduced Fat Cheesy Potato Soup

3   cups diced raw
    potatoes
¾   cup diced celery
¾   cup diced carrots
1   tablespoon minced
    onion
1   teaspoon parsley
    flakes

2   cups water
    salt and pepper to taste
1   can reduced fat cream
    of chicken soup
2   cups skim milk
½   pound light
    Velveeta cheese,
    cubed

Combine potatoes, celery, carrots, onion, parsley, water, salt and pepper in a large kettle. Bring to a boil; reduce heat. Simmer for 20 minutes or until vegetables are tender. Stir in cream of chicken soup, milk, and cheese. Heat until cheese is melted, stirring frequently.

Yield: 10 servings
❧ *Calories: 155*
❧ *Fat: 5 grams*

Reduced Fat Macaroni and Cheese Soup

1 cup elbow macaroni	2 tablespoons chicken-flavored bouillon granules
¼ cup reduced fat margarine	½ teaspoon white pepper
½ cup finely chopped carrots	2 tablespoons cornstarch
½ cup finely chopped celery	2 tablespoons water
1 small onion, finely chopped	1 (8-ounce) can whole kernel corn, drained
4 cups skim milk	½ cup frozen English peas
8 ounces processed fat free American cheese slices	

Cook macaroni according to package directions, omitting salt. Drain and rinse. In large skillet, melt margarine and add carrots, celery, and onion. Cook, stirring constantly until tender. In heavy Dutch oven, combine milk and cheese slices. Cook until cheese melts. Add bouillon granules and pepper. Combine cornstarch and water; stir into milk mixture. Cook over medium heat, stirring constantly, until mixture thickens. Boil 1 minute, stirring constantly. Stir in macaroni and vegetable mixture; add corn and English peas. Cook over low heat until hot.

Yield: 8 servings
❦ Calories: 180   ❦ Fat: 2 grams

Low Fat Taco Soup

1½ pounds lean ground beef
2   onions, chopped
1   green bell pepper, chopped
3   cloves garlic, crushed or 2 tablespoons minced garlic
red pepper to taste
lemon pepper to taste
Tabasco Pepper Sauce to taste
1   package taco seasoning
1   package (or 2 tablespoons) dry Italian seasoning

1   can pinto beans
1   can pinto beans with jalapenos
1   can Rotel tomatoes, chopped
1   can stewed tomatoes, chopped
2   small cans tomato sauce
1   can white hominy, drained
1   can whole kernel corn, drained
4   cups water

Sauté beef, onions, bell pepper and garlic. Drain excess fat and add remaining ingredients. Bring to a boil; reduce heat and simmer for one hour. Remove from heat and let stand 3-4 hours. To serve, garnish with chopped green onion and low-fat cheese. (Cheese for garnishing not included in nutritional information) *This soup freezes well!

Yield: 20 servings of 1 cup each
❣ *Calories: 125*
❣ *Fat: 3 grams*

Low Fat Potato Soup

6	cups red potatoes, peeled and sliced	1½-2	quarts water
4	cups onions, sliced	1	cup skim milk
4	teaspoons powdered chicken broth or 5 bouillon cubes	1	bunch green onions, finely sliced
			salt and pepper to taste

Place potatoes and onions in large pot. Add water to cover and bring to a boil. Reduce heat and simmer, partially covered, for 45 minutes. When potatoes are tender, transfer with onions and water to food processor in batches and process until smooth. Return to pot and add remaining ingredients except green onions, cooking until thoroughly heated. Top with green onions and serve.

Yield: 12 servings
❦ *Calories: 95*
❦ *Fat: ½ gram*

Low Fat Chicken Florentine Soup

The long grain wild rice called for in this recipe is high in sodium. If you are on a low sodium diet, omit boxed rice and substitute 6 cups brown rice and Italian seasoning.

4-6 boneless skinless chicken breasts, cooked and chopped
1 can fat free chicken broth
1½ cups frozen vegetable blend (onion, bell pepper, celery)
2 tablespoons margarine
4-5 tablespoons flour
3 cups skim milk
2 (10-ounce) packages frozen chopped spinach
1 cup chopped fresh mushrooms or 1 (4-ounce) can sliced mushrooms
2 (6-ounce) boxes long grain wild rice

Boil chicken in 1 can fat free chicken broth; add water to cover. Reserve 4 cups of chicken broth. Sauté frozen onion blend in margarine until tender; add broth to sauté if needed. Whisk in the flour and cook for 1 minute, stirring constantly. Remove from the heat. In a large bowl mix the milk and warm chicken broth (4 cups). Slowly add the milk mixture to the sautéed onion and flour mixture, stirring until blended. Stir in the spinach, mushrooms, and rice with seasoning packets. Return to the stovetop. Simmer for about 30 minutes or until rice is tender, stirring frequently. Add liquid as needed for broth.

Yield: 18 servings
❦ *Calories: 180* ❦ *Fat: 2 grams*

Reduced Fat Chicken and Sausage Gumbo

When making gumbo, the base is called a roux. The traditional method of making a roux is to brown flour in a skillet with oil, which adds a significant amount of calories and fat. You'll never miss the fat and calories using this method. Isn't it great to be able to "Eat What You Love" without the guilt?

1   cup flour*
1½ pounds chicken (boneless, skinless)
½   pound link sausage (reduced fat turkey sausage)
1½ cups onions, chopped
½   cup celery, chopped
½   cup green bell pepper, chopped
½   cup green onions, chopped
8   cups hot water
1   teaspoon salt
½   teaspoon ground red pepper
2   bay leaves
1   chicken bouillon cube
2   tablespoons parsley
½   tablespoon garlic
2   teaspoons Cajun seasoning (i.e. Tony's Chachere's Original Seasoning)
½   teaspoons dried thyme
1   teaspoon hot sauce

(Continued on next page.)

Place flour in a 13 × 9 × 2-inch pan. Bake at 400° for 15 minutes or until caramel-colored, stirring every 5 minutes. *An envelope of fat free brown gravy mix may be used in place of cooked flour. Brown chicken over medium heat in a Dutch oven coated with nonstick cooking spray. Add sausage, stirring to brown. Remove sausage and chicken and set aside. Sauté vegetables, except for green onions, in Dutch oven until tender; sprinkle with cooked flour. Gradually stir in water; bring to a boil. Add chicken, sausage, and seasonings, except parsley. Reduce heat; simmer uncovered for 1 hour. Cook gumbo, uncovered, 30 minutes. Stir in green onions and parsley, cook uncovered an additional 5 minutes. Remove and discard bay leaves; serve over rice.

Yield: 8 servings of about 1 cup each
❦ *Calories: 180*
❦ *Fat: 5 grams*

Fat Free Cream of Broccoli Soup

2-3 tablespoons liquid Butter Buds
1 cup chopped onion
2½ tablespoons flour
½ teaspoon salt
½ teaspoon pepper
2 cups nonfat chicken broth
10 ounces frozen chopped broccoli, thawed and drained
2 cups skim milk

Sauté onion in Butter Buds over low heat about 10 minutes. Add flour, salt, and pepper and stir constantly for 2 minutes. Add broth slowly. Add broccoli. Bring to a boil, stirring frequently. Cover and simmer until broccoli is tender. Puree in blender. Return to pan; add milk and bring to simmer.

Yield: 4 servings
ᵛ *Calories: 100*
ᵛ *Fat: 0 grams*

Reduced Fat Sunburst Chicken Salad

1 tablespoon fat free mayonnaise

1 tablespoon fat free sour cream

2 teaspoons frozen orange juice concentrate, thawed

¼ teaspoon grated orange peel

1 boneless skinless chicken breast (6 ounces),cooked and coarsely chopped

1 large kiwi, peeled and thinly sliced

⅓ cup tangerine or mandarin orange sections, halved

¼ cup finely chopped celery

4 lettuce leaves, washed

2 tablespoons cashews, coarsely chopped

In small bowl, combine mayonnaise, sour cream, orange juice concentrate, and orange peel until well blended. Add chicken, kiwi, tangerine, and celery; toss to coat. Cover and refrigerate 2 hours before serving. Spoon chicken mixture over lettuce leaves and top each serving evenly with cashews. Add additional garnish as desired.

Yield: 2 servings
❦ *Calories: 195*
❦ *Fat: 6 grams*

Reduced Fat Southwestern Chicken Salad

4   boneless skinless chicken breasts (or enough to equal 4 cups)
fajita seasoning to taste
¼   cup light mayonnaise
²/₃ cup fat free sour cream
1   teaspoon chili powder
½   teaspoon ground cumin
¼   teaspoon dried basil
salt and pepper to taste
Tabasco Pepper Sauce to taste

½   cup shredded reduced fat sharp cheddar cheese
½   cup chopped green onion
1   package fresh mushrooms, sliced
1   head lettuce, shredded (romaine, iceberg, etc.)
2   medium tomatoes, chopped
2   tablespoons real bacon bits

Season chicken with fajita seasoning and cook. Cut into bite-sized pieces. Blend mayonnaise, sour cream, chili powder, cumin, basil, salt, pepper and Tabasco. Set aside. Combine chicken, cheddar cheese, green onion, and mushrooms. Toss with mayonnaise mixture until well coated. Refrigerate for 2 hours. Serve on a bed of shredded lettuce topped with chopped tomatoes and bacon bits.

Yield: 6 servings
❦ *Calories: 355*
❦ *Fat: 6½ grams*

Party Chicken Salad

*This salad is wonderfully displayed
when stuffed in a tomato shell.
Serve with low fat or fat free crackers.
It is also a delicious sandwich filling.*

4   boneless skinless
    chicken breasts
1   red apple, chopped
3-4 tablespoons sweet
    pickle relish
1   cup seedless white
    grapes, sliced

⅓   cup fat free
    mayonnaise
⅓   cup light salad
    dressing
Nature's seasons
⅓   cup toasted almonds,
    sliced, or ⅓ cup
    toasted pecans,
    chopped

Boil chicken and chop into bite-sized pieces. Set aside. Combine apple, relish, and grapes in mixing bowl. Add cooled chicken. Gently stir in mayonnaise and dressing until salad reaches desired consistency. Season to taste. Add toasted almonds or pecans just before serving.

Yield: 12 servings
❦ *Calories: 125*
❦ *Fat: 5 grams*

Low Fat Pasta and Fruit Chicken Salad

6   ounces uncooked rotini or elbow macaroni
½   cup fat free mayonnaise
½   cup light salad dressing
½   teaspoon paprika
¾   teaspoon Nature's seasons
2   cups cooked chicken, cubed or 3 (5-ounce) cans 98% fat free white chicken packed in water

1   cup seedless white grapes, halved
1   (11-ounce) can mandarin oranges
1   (20-ounce) can pineapple chunks, drained

Cook pasta to desired firmness according to package directions. While pasta is cooking, combine mayonnaise, salad dressing, paprika, and seasoning in large bowl. Blend well. Drain pasta; rinse with cold water to cool. Add pasta, chicken, grapes, oranges, and pineapple to mayonnaise mixture; mix gently to coat. Cover; refrigerate 1 hour to blend flavors.

Yield: 9 servings of about 1 cup each
☽ *Calories: 245*
☽ *Fat: 4 grams*

Low Fat Exotic Chicken Salad

½ cup reduced fat mayonnaise
2 teaspoons mustard
2 cups chopped cooked chicken or 2 (10-ounce) cans 97% fat free chicken breast
½ cup chopped celery
½ cup chopped mushrooms
¼ cup chopped green bell pepper

1 (20-ounce) can pineapple chunks canned in juice, drained
1 cup red seedless grapes, halved
1 (11-ounce) can mandarin oranges, drained
salt and pepper to taste

Garnish: (not included in nutritional information)

⅓ cup sliced almonds, toasted

green leafy lettuce
croutons

Mix mayonnaise and mustard with chicken in large bowl. Add vegetables and mix well. Chill. Before serving, add fruits and mix gently before serving. Garnish as desired.

Yield: 8 servings
❦ *Calories: 215*
❦ *Fat: 5 grams*

Low Fat Hot Chicken Salad

2   cups chicken breast, cooked and chopped
1   can reduced fat cream of chicken soup
1   cup diced celery
2   teaspoons minced onion
1   tablespoon lemon juice
½   teaspoon salt
¼   teaspoon pepper
4   tablespoons reduced fat margarine
1½ cup baked potato chips, crushed

Mix all ingredients and place in casserole dish. Sprinkle with crushed potato chips. Bake at 350° for about 30 minutes.

Yield: 12 servings
❦ *Calories: 100*
❦ *Fat: 3½ grams*

Low Fat Oriental Chicken Salad

$^2/_3$ cup reduced fat mayonnaise
¼ teaspoon salt
¼ teaspoon curry powder
¼ teaspoon soy sauce
3 boneless skinless chicken breasts, cooked and cubed
1 small can water chestnuts, sliced or chopped

½ cup celery, sliced or chopped
¼ cup toasted almond slices
1½ cup seedless white grapes, sliced

Cream mayonnaise, salt, curry powder, and soy sauce together in small bowl; set aside. In larger bowl, combine chicken, water chestnuts, and celery and add mayonnaise mixture. Chill. Stir in almonds and grapes just before serving.

Yield: 9 servings
❦ *Calories: 115*
❦ *Fat: 4 grams*

Low Fat Chicken Spaghetti Salad

4   boneless skinless chicken breasts
8-10 cherry tomatoes, halved
1   (8-ounce) package vermicelli whole wheat spaghetti, boiled in broth

1   cup chopped broccoli florets, cooked and cut up
½   chopped purple onion (optional)

Dressing:

¾   cup commercial light Italian salad dressing
1   teaspoon basil
1   teaspoon Beau Monde seasoning

1   tablespoon lemon juice
dash of salt

Combine salad ingredients. In separate bowl, mix dressing ingredients until well blended and pour over spaghetti mixture. Refrigerate overnight. May add grated cheese just before serving.

Yield: 10 servings of 1 cup each
❦ *Calories: 215*
❦ *Fat: 2½ grams*

Low Fat Confetti-Pasta Salad

1   (8-ounce) package small shell macaroni, uncooked
3   cups fresh broccoli florets
1   small (5-6 ounces) can pitted ripe olives, drained
1   sweet red pepper, diced
1   yellow pepper, diced
1   green bell pepper, diced
1   small package frozen green peas
1   cup small cherry tomatoes, sliced
2-3 stalks celery, sliced or diced
2   small yellow squash, sliced or diced
4   carrots, scraped and diced
¼   cup thinly sliced green onions
¼   cup fat free Parmesan cheese
1   cup lean chopped ham

Dressing:

8   ounces fat free Caesar dressing
4   ounces light Ranch dressing

Cook macaroni according to package directions until tender; drain. Do not overcook. Rinse with cold water and drain. Place ½ of cooked pasta in serving bowl. Divide other ingredients and layer half of each over pasta. Combine dressing and drizzle ½ over salad; then repeat layers with remaining pasta and other ingredients. Top with remaining salad dressing. Cover and chill at least 8 hours. Toss gently before serving.

Yield: 15 servings of 1 cup each
❦ *Calories: 160*   ❦ *Fat: 4 grams*

Hearty Low Fat Macaroni Salad

2 cups cooked chicken, cubed
2 cups cooked ham, cubed
2 cups cooked salad shrimp
1 (7-ounce) package macaroni shells, cooked and drained
1 rib celery, sliced
¼ cup diced green bell pepper
¼ cup diced sweet red pepper
¼ cup diced onion
1 teaspoon salt
½ teaspoon pepper

Dressing:

½ cup reduced fat mayonnaise
½ cup light sour cream
2 tablespoons vinegar
½ teaspoon granulated sugar
2 teaspoons minced fresh dill or 1 teaspoon dill weed

In a large bowl, toss the chicken, ham, shrimp, macaroni, celery, peppers, onion, salt, and pepper. In a separate bowl, combine all dressing ingredients and mix well. Pour over salad and toss. Cover and chill for 3-4 hours.

Yield: 15 servings of 1 cup each
❦ *Calories: 165*
❦ *Fat: 2 grams*

Wonderful Low Fat Turkey Salad

Try serving this salad in a tomato shell with low fat crackers. White chicken may be substituted for turkey.

2 cups diced cooked white turkey

¼ cup reduced fat cream of chicken soup

4 ounces low fat cream cheese

½ cup fat free non dairy liquid coffee creamer

1 cup finely chopped celery

1½ cups white seedless grapes, halved

¼ cup sliced almonds, toasted

1 cup fat free mayonnaise

1 teaspoon salt

¼ teaspoon pepper

Combine drained cooked turkey and cream of chicken soup. If turkey is dry, add up to ¼ cup water. In separate bowl cream liquid creamer with cream cheese until a whipping consistency. In large bowl combine turkey, cream cheese mixture, celery, grapes, almonds, mayonnaise, salt, and pepper.

Yield: 12 servings of ½ cup each
🐦 *Calories: 87*
🐦 *Fat: 2.4 grams*

Light Tuna Fish Salad

3 small cans light tuna in water
½ cup reduced fat mayonnaise
1-2 tablespoons sweet pickle relish

1 red apple, chopped
3 boiled egg whites
1 boiled egg yolk

Mix all ingredients in a bowl. Serve as a sandwich or with crackers.

Yield: 8 servings of ½ cup each
❦ *Calories: 130*
❦ *Fat: 6 grams*

Low Fat Tuna Cheese Salad

Serve this creamy salad on wheat bread or low fat/fat free crackers. Or, try it as a dip with raw vegetables!

6-8 ounces fat free cream cheese
1 can (6⅛ ounces) tuna packed in water
2 tablespoons fat free mayonnaise
1 tablespoon lemon juice
¾ teaspoon curry powder
dash salt
2 green onions, finely sliced

Soften cream cheese at room temperature for about one hour, or soften in microwave. Drain tuna; mash with fork. In medium bowl, combine cream cheese, tuna, and mayonnaise. Add lemon juice, curry, and salt. Mix to blend well. Add onions and stir well. Chill for 1 hour to blend flavors.

Yield: 4 servings
❦ *Calories: 105*
❦ *Fat: less than 1 gram*

Reduced Fat Island Salad

*During my second pregnancy,
with Elizabeth-Kate, I craved salads — not just
ordinary green salads, but extraordinary salads.
This was one of my favorites. Elizabeth-Kate
has always loved salads, too.*

½ cup cashews
½ cup peanuts
¼ cup sesame seeds
¼ cup poppy seeds
2 ribs celery, diced
1 cup raisins
1 banana, diced
2 carrots, diced
1 red apple, diced

3 green onions, chopped
1 cup broccoli, chopped
1 (1-pound) bag shredded cabbage (coleslaw mix)
1 cup Italian vinaigrette dressing

Combine all ingredients, except dressing, in a large serving bowl. Add the dressing and toss to coat. Serve immediately.

Yield: 24 servings
❧ *Calories: 110*
❧ *Fat: 5 grams*

Reduced Fat Mardi Gras Salad

This tangy salad may be stored up to two weeks in refrigerator. For alternate sauce, use 8 ounces fat free red wine vinegar dressing, 1 cup sugar, and salt and pepper to taste.

1 can French style or wax beans, drained	2 bunches green onions
1 cup chopped green bell pepper	1 can shoe-peg corn, drained
1 can small sweet peas, drained	1 small jar pimentos, drained
	1 cup chopped celery

Sauce:

1 cup granulated sugar	1 teaspoon pepper
1 teaspoon salt	¼ cup cooking oil
¾ cup vinegar	

Toss salad ingredients in a large bowl. To prepare sauce, combine ingredients in saucepan and bring to a boil. Remove from heat and let cool. Pour over vegetable mixture and place all in covered container. Refrigerate overnight; drain sauce to serve.

*Nutritional information based on fat free red wine vinegar dressing.

Yield: 12 servings of ½ cup each
❦ *Calories: 80*
❦ *Fat: 0 grams*

Deliciously Different Reduced Fat Broccoli Salad

2 large bunches broccoli, washed and drained
1 cup raisins, regular or golden
8 tablespoons real bacon bits
½ cup sunflower seeds or cashews
1 cup shredded reduced fat cheddar cheese

Dressing:

½ cup fat free mayonnaise
⅓ cup fat free red wine vinegar dressing

Chop broccoli well and place in large bowl. Add remaining salad ingredients. In smaller bowl, combine mayonnaise and dressing and mix well with whisk. Pour over broccoli mixture and toss well. Refrigerate for at least one hour before serving.

Yield: 16 servings of ½ cup each
❦ *Calories: 115*
❦ *Fat: 3 grams*

Low Fat Mexican Salad

1 (15-ounce) can ranch style beans, washed and drained
2-3 sliced jalapeno peppers
8 ounces shredded fat free cheddar cheese
1 teaspoon chili powder
1 teaspoon ground cumin
1 small bunch green onions, chopped
1 head lettuce, shredded
1 tomato, chopped
1 bag (8-9 ounces) baked tortilla chips
1 small bottle fat free Catalina dressing

Toss together beans, jalapenos, cheese, and seasonings in large bowl. Add onions, lettuce, and tomato to mix. Just before serving, add chips and dressing.

Yield: 10 servings
❦ *Calories: 225*
❦ *Fat: 1.5 grams*

Modified Blueberry Salad

2 small boxes sugar free raspberry gelatin
2 cups boiling water
1 (15-ounce) can blueberries in light syrup, drained (reserve juice)
1 (8¼-ounce) can crushed pineapple in its own juice, drained (reserve juice)

8 ounces fat free cream cheese
½ cup granulated sugar
8 ounces light sour cream
½ teaspoon vanilla extract
⅛ cup chopped pecans

Dissolve gelatin in boiling water. Mix juices of blueberry and pineapple together, and add enough water to make 2 cups. Add to gelatin. Stir in blueberries and pineapple. Pour into 2-quart shallow pan and refrigerate until set. Combine cream cheese, sugar, sour cream and vanilla. Spread over gelatin layer; sprinkle pecans on top.

Yield: 12 servings
❦ *Calories: 120*
❦ *Fat: less than 1 gram*

Low Fat Orange "Spooky Salad"

*Great anytime, but especially festive-
looking at Halloween.*

3 cups water
1 (3-ounce) box sugar free orange gelatin
1 (3.4-ounce) box fat free instant vanilla pudding mix
1 (3-ounce) box tapioca pudding mix
1 (15-ounce) can mandarin oranges, drained
1 (8-ounce) can crushed pineapple, drained
8 ounces fat free Cool Whip, thawed
½ cup flaked coconut
¼ cup chopped pecans
1½ cups miniature marshmallows
raisins to decorate

In medium saucepan, bring water to a boil. Whisk in gelatin and pudding mixes. Return to a boil, stirring constantly; and boil for 1 minute. Remove from heat and cool completely. Fold in oranges, pineapple, Cool Whip, coconut, pecans, and marshmallows. Spoon into a serving bowl. Cover and refrigerate 2 hours. Use raisins to decorate as a jack-o-lantern.

Yield: 14 servings
❦ *Calories: 150*
❦ *Fat: 2¼ grams*

Fat Free Pistachio Salad

This quick and easy salad is already a holiday favorite. Make it healthier this year with the recipe below.

1   (3.4-ounce) box pistachio instant pudding mix
1   cup miniature marshmallows
1   small container fat free Cool Whip

8   ounces fat free cottage cheese
1   (15¼-ounce) can crushed pineapple in its own juice, drained

Combine all ingredients and mix well. Chill in refrigerator before serving.

Yield: 12 servings of ½ cup each
❦ *Calories: 110*
❦ *Fat: 0 grams*

Low Fat Frozen Salad

3   bananas, sliced or
    mashed
1   (8-ounce) can crushed
    pineapple in its
    own juice
14-18 packets sugar
    substitute
8   ounces fat free
    sour cream

¼   cup chopped pecans
½   cup cherries, sliced
8   ounces fat free
    Cool Whip
1   (16-ounce) can light
    fruit cocktail in
    extra-light syrup,
    drained

Combine all ingredients and mix well. Place in shallow pan and freeze. Cut into 30 servings.

Yield: 30 servings
❧ *Calories: 62*
❧ *Fat: 3 grams (omit pecans for a fat free salad)*

Fat Free 5-Fruit Salad

2 cans light fruit cocktail, with juice
1 can light peach pie filling, with juice
1 can mandarin oranges, with juice

4 bananas, sliced
4 cups strawberries, sliced

Combine all ingredients in large serving bowl and mix well. Chill in refrigerator 4-6 hours or overnight before serving.

Yield: 24 servings
❦ *Calories: 65*
❦ *Fat: 0 grams*

Fat Free Fruit Salad

1 large box sugar free strawberry gelatin

1 (16-ounce) can pineapple tidbits in juice

1 pound fat free cottage cheese

1 large container light Cool Whip

In a small saucepan over low heat, mix dry gelatin with pineapple and juice. Stir until gelatin is dissolved. In a large bowl, combine cottage cheese and gelatin mixture; fold in Cool Whip. Serve immediately as a fruit dip, or refrigerate and serve as a congealed salad.

Yield: 24 servings
❦ *Calories: 57*
❦ *Fat: 0 grams*

Yogurt Fruit Dressing

¼ cup granulated sugar
8 teaspoons cornstarch
2 cups pineapple juice

½ cup lemon juice
½ cup orange juice
1 cup plain nonfat yogurt

Combine sugar, cornstarch, and juices in double boiler and cook until thickened, stirring constantly. Allow to cool. Fold in yogurt. Serve with fresh fruit.

Yield: 15 servings of 2 tablespoons each
❦ *Calories: 30*
❦ *Fat: 0 grams*

Reduced Fat Cornbread Salad

1 package Mexican cornbread mix, baked according to package directions

1 (16-ounce) can pinto beans with jalapenos, rinsed and drained

1 (11-ounce) can whole kernel Mexican-style corn, drained

1 large tomato, chopped

½ cup chopped green onions

½ green bell pepper, chopped

1 ounce real bacon bits

1 tablespoon dry Hidden Valley Ranch salad dressing mix

8 ounces light Velveeta cheese or 8 ounces light Cheese Whiz

½ can Rotel tomatoes

Crumble layer of cornbread in bottom of dish. Combine beans, corn, tomato, onions, bell pepper, bacon bits, and dressing mix and pour over cornbread. In a saucepan or in the microwave, melt cheese, add Rotel and mix well. Pour over top. Repeat layers until mixture is gone. For best flavor, chill overnight.

Yield: 12 servings of ½ cup each
🍅 *Calories: 165*
🍅 *Fat: 4 grams*

Low Fat Cornbread Dressing

To make cornbread, use 1 small package of cornbread mix. Prepare according to directions, substituting skim milk and Egg Beaters. Spray skillet with nonstick cooking spray.

½　onion, chopped
2-3 celery stalks,
　　chopped
2　　cans fat free
　　chicken broth

1　　(8-inch) pan
　　cornbread
4-5 green onions,
　　chopped
¼　cup fat free Egg
　　Beaters

Sauté onion and celery in 1 cup chicken broth until tender. Crumble cornbread into a mixing bowl; add sautéed onions and celery, green onions, and Egg Beaters. Mix well, adding enough broth to reduce dryness. Bake at 375° for 20-30 minutes until brown.

Yield: 6 servings
❦ *Calories: 150*
❦ *Fat: 2½ grams*

Stacey's Fat Free Mexican Cornbread

1½ cups yellow cornmeal
2 teaspoons baking powder
2 egg whites
1 cup fat free sour cream
⅓ cup fat free yogurt
2 cups shredded fat free cheddar cheese
1 cup whole kernel corn
1 bunch green onions, chopped
3 large jalapeno peppers
¼ cup chopped green bell pepper
½ cup chopped red pepper
1 (4-ounce) can green chilies

Combine cornmeal, baking powder, and egg whites in large bowl. Stir in sour cream, yogurt, cheddar cheese, and corn. Add green onions, peppers, and green chilies to batter; stir until moistened. Pour mixture into a large skillet coated with cooking spray. Bake at 400° for 45 minutes or until golden brown.

Yield: 16 servings
❦ *Calories: 100*
❦ *Fat: 0*

Fat Free Banana Bread

1⅓ cups plain flour
¼ teaspoon baking powder
½ teaspoon salt
1 cup granulated sugar
⅓ cup liquid Butter Buds

½ cup fat free Egg Beaters
4 medium bananas, mashed

Combine dry ingredients. Add sugar, Butter Buds, Egg Beaters, and bananas. Pour into loaf pan prepared with nonstick cooking spray. Bake at 350° for 35 minutes or until done.

Yield: 16 servings
❧ *Calories: 115*
❧ *Fat: 0 grams*

Low Fat Hawaiian Bread

1 (14-ounce) box banana quick bread mix	¾ cup fat free Egg Beaters
1 (15.6-ounce) box cranberry quick bread mix	2 mashed ripe bananas 1 cup thin flaked coconut
2 cups skim milk	⅓ cup sliced almonds
5 tablespoons light applesauce	

Preheat oven to 350°. Spray 2 loaf pans with nonstick spray and set aside. Combine mixes, milk, applesauce, and Egg Beaters in large mixing bowl. Stir until mixture is moistened. Fold in bananas, coconut, and almonds. Pour batter into prepared pans. Bake at 350° for 45-60 minutes.

Yield: 24 servings (12 per loaf)
❦ *Calories: 190*
❦ *Fat: 3 fat grams*

Low Fat Cheesy Seafood Bread

4 ounces fat free cream cheese, softened

2 tablespoons reduced fat margarine

1 (4-ounce) can chopped green chilies, drained

1 (4-ounce) can small shrimp, drained

1 (4-ounce) can crabmeat, drained

1 tablespoon lemon juice

1 tablespoon Worcestershire sauce

Tony Chachere's Original Seasoning to taste

1 cup shredded reduced fat sharp cheddar cheese

sliced French bread

Garnish:

fat free sour cream   green onions

In a mixing bowl, blend cream cheese and margarine together. Add chilies, shrimp, crabmeat, lemon juice, Worcestershire sauce, seasonings, and ½ cup cheese. Spread mixture evenly on French bread slices. Bake at 350° for 10-15 minutes. Remove and sprinkle with remaining cheese. Bake about 5 minutes or until cheese is melted. Garnish with sour cream and onions and serve.

Yield: 14 servings
❦ *Calories: 165*
❦ *Fat: 3 grams*

Low Fat Spicy Apple Muffins

1⅔ cups all-purpose flour
3 tablespoons granulated sugar
2½ teaspoons baking powder
1 teaspoon ground cinnamon
½ teaspoon ground nutmeg
¼ teaspoon salt
1 egg, beaten
1 cup skim milk
2 tablespoons margarine
1 cup finely chopped apple

Combine flour, sugar, baking powder, cinnamon, nutmeg, and salt in a large bowl; make a well in center of mixture. Combine egg, milk, and margarine; pour into center of dry ingredients, stirring just until moistened. Fold in apple. Coat muffin pans with nonstick spray. Spoon batter into pans, filling half full. Bake at 400° for 25 minutes.

Yield: 1 dozen muffins
❦ *Calories: 91*
❦ *Fat: 1 gram*

Fat Free Harvest Apple Muffins

1¾ cups all-purpose flour
1   tablespoon baking powder
½   teaspoon salt
¾   cup granulated sugar
2   egg whites

⅓   cup applesauce
⅓   cup low fat buttermilk
1   teaspoon cinnamon
1   teaspoon butter extract
3   cups chopped apples, with skin

Preheat oven to 400°. In a large bowl, combine dry ingredients, including sugar. Make a well in the center and set aside. In a small bowl, beat egg whites until foamy. Stir in applesauce, buttermilk, cinnamon, and extract. Add to flour mixture and stir just until moistened. Fold in apples. Spoon batter into prepared (12-cup) muffin pan. Bake for 20-22 minutes.

Yield: 12 servings
❦ *Calories: 130*
❦ *Fat: less than one gram*

Reduced Fat Breakfast Pizza

1 (10.5-ounce)
   package 97% fat
   free sausage
1 package reduced
   fat crescent rolls
1 cup hash browns
6 slices fat free sharp
   cheddar cheese
4 egg whites and
   1 egg yolk

½ cup fat free Egg
   Beaters
¼ cup skim milk
salt to taste
½ teaspoon pepper
½ cup fat free
   mozzarella cheese

Brown sausage in skillet sprayed with nonstick cooking spray. Separate rolls into 8 pieces in ungreased 12-inch pizza pan. Press rolls to form crust, covering bottom and sides of pan. Sprinkle sausage and potatoes over crust and top with cheddar cheese. In mixing bowl, beat eggs, Egg Beaters, milk, salt, and pepper. Pour over crust. Sprinkle mozzarella cheese on top. Bake at 375° for 40 minutes. If top begins to overbrown, reduce heat to 350°.

Yield: 12 servings
❦ *Calories: 70*
❦ *Fat: 6 grams*

Everybody's Favorite Spinach

For a great casserole, add 1 cup cooked brown rice and 1 (10-ounce) can of chicken. Each serving is about 165 calories and 5 fat grams.

2 (10-ounce) packages frozen chopped spinach	½ cup shredded reduced fat sharp cheddar cheese
½ (10-ounce) can reduced fat cream of mushroom soup	2 tablespoons grated onion
½ cup reduced fat mayonnaise	12 reduced fat cheese crackers, crushed

Cook spinach according to package directions; drain. Place in a shallow baking dish. Combine soup, mayonnaise, cheese and onion in a small bowl and mix well. Pour over spinach. Sprinkle with crushed crackers. Bake for 20 minutes.

Yield: 8 Servings.
❦ Calories: 85
❦ Fat: 3 grams

Reduced Fat Stuffed Squash

4 yellow squash
1 tablespoon reduced fat margarine
½ cup 97% fat free pork sausage
½ cup onion
½ cup bread crumbs
½ cup reduced fat shredded cheddar cheese
½ cup light sour cream
1-2 tablespoons parsley

Cut squash into halves. Scrape and remove pulp. Add margarine and sauté squash and onions until tender. Cook sausage. Combine squash and remaining ingredients. Spoon mixture into shells. Sprinkle with parsley. Bake at 375° for 20-25 minutes.

Yield: 8 servings
❦ *Calories: 110*
❦ *Fat: 4 grams*

Fat Free Stuffed Potatoes

3	medium baking potatoes	3	green onions, chopped
1	cup fat free cheddar cheese	3	tablespoons red diced pimentos
1	cup fat free sour cream	1	teaspoon cumin
1	egg white	⅛	teaspoon black pepper
2	tablespoons fat free margarine		

Wash potatoes, prick with fork, and bake or microwave until done. Let cool. Cut potatoes in half and scoop out pulp, leaving shells intact. Set shells aside. Mix all ingredients together in bowl until well blended. Stuff shells with potato mixture and place on an ungreased baking sheet. Bake for 10 minutes at 375°.

Yield: 6 servings
❧ *Calories: 130*
❧ *Fat: 0 grams*

Sweet Potato Yum Yum Casserole

3 cups cooked sweet potatoes	1 teaspoon vanilla extract
⅓ cup granulated sugar	1 teaspoon butter extract
½ cup liquid Butter Buds	⅓ cup skim milk
3 egg whites	

Topping:

½ cup light brown sugar	⅓ cup chopped pecans
½ cup flour	

Boil and mash potatoes. Combine all ingredients and mix well. Place mixture in 13 × 9-inch casserole dish prepared with nonstick cooking spray. Combine topping ingredients and sprinkle over sweet potato mixture. Bake at 350° for about 35 minutes.

Yield: 12 servings
❧ *Calories: 140*
❧ *Fat: 2 grams*

Victoria's Favorite Casserole

1   (15-ounce) can
    sweet peas
1   can asparagus
1   can mushrooms
1   (8-ounce) can water
    chestnuts

1   (10¾-ounce) can
    reduced fat cream
    of mushroom soup
red pepper
½   cup shredded low
    fat sharp cheddar
    cheese

Spray a casserole dish with nonstick cooking spray.
Drain vegetables and layer in casserole. Top with
mushroom soup. Sprinkle with red pepper to taste.
Cover with grated cheese. Bake at 350° until bubbly.

Yield: 8 servings
❦ *Calories: 85*
❦ *Fat: 2 grams*

Reduced Fat Cheesy Green Bean Casserole

8 ounces light sour cream	3 cans fresh cut green beans, drained
1 jar light Cheese Whiz, melted	⅓ cup sliced almonds

Blend sour cream and melted cheese well; add to drained green beans in casserole dish. Top with sliced almonds. Bake at 350° until bubbly.

Yield: 12 servings
❦ *Calories: 115*
❦ *Fat: 5 grams*

Low Fat Quick and Easy Corn Casserole

1 can whole kernel corn, drained	½ cup fat free Egg Beaters
1 can cream style corn	¼ cup reduced calorie margarine
2 tablespoons flour	

Combine ingredients and bake at 400° for 30 minutes.

Yield: 6 servings
❦ *Calories: 130*
❦ *Fat: 3½ grams*

Low Fat Three Bean & Wild Rice Casserole

1 tablespoon margarine
4 medium-size carrots, cut into ¼ inch slices
1 large onion, thinly sliced
1 (10-ounce) package mushrooms, cut into ¼ inch slices
salt to taste
1 (10¾-ounce) can reduced fat cream of mushroom soup
3¼ cups water
1 (6-ounce) box wild rice
1 (15¼ to 19-ounce) can red kidney beans, rinsed and drained
1 (16 to 19-ounce) can Great Northern beans or white kidney beans, rinsed and drained
1 can pinto beans
½ teaspoon coarsely ground black pepper

In 12-inch skillet over medium-high heat, melt margarine and cook carrots, onion, and mushrooms until vegetables are golden, adding salt to taste. Meanwhile, in 2-quart saucepan, heat cream of mushroom soup and 3¼ cups water to boiling. In deep 2½-quart casserole, combine carrot mixture, hot soup mixture, and wild rice. Cover and bake at 400° for 1 hour. Stir beans and pepper into casserole. Cover and bake 20 minutes longer or until hot. Stir before serving.

Yield: 9 servings of 1 cup each
❦ *Calories: 260*
❦ *Fat: 2 grams*

Low Fat Black Bean Casserole Ole'

1 pound dried black beans or 3 (15-ounce) cans black beans	2 stalks celery, diced
	1 can whole kernel corn
1 (10-ounce) can Rotel tomatoes	2 teaspoons chili powder
1 (14-ounce) can stewed tomatoes	1 teaspoon cumin
	parsley
1 (4-ounce) can green chilies	salt to taste
1 (4-ounce) can black olives	1 cup corn meal
	1½ cup skim milk
1 cup diced onion	⅓ cup shredded cheddar cheese

Soak and cook black beans until soft. Combine all other ingredients in a 9 × 13-inch baking dish. Top with cheese. Bake at 350° for 45 minutes.

Yield: 20 servings
❦ *Fat: 1 gram*
❦ *Calories: 110*

Low Fat Corn Casserole

1 medium onion, chopped	2 jalapeno peppers or 5 slices, chopped
3 cups cooked rice	1 tablespoon granulated sugar
2 cans cream style corn	½ cup shredded reduced fat cheddar cheese
1 can whole kernel corn, drained	

Spray skillet with nonstick cooking spray. Add onion and sauté. Stir in rice, corn, peppers, and sugar. Place mixture in casserole dish and heat at 350° for 25 minutes. Top with shredded cheese and heat until cheese melts.

Yield: 14 servings of ½ cup each
❦ *Calories: 100*
❦ *Fat: 1 gram*

Low Fat Potato Casserole

¼ cup reduced fat margarine
1 medium onion, chopped
1 cup reduced fat cream of mushroom soup
1 teaspoon parsley
salt and pepper to taste
1 cup fat free sour cream
½ cup fat free shredded cheddar cheese
½ cup reduced fat shredded cheddar cheese
1 (32-ounce) package frozen hash brown potatoes, thawed
1 cup corn flaked cereal, crushed

Combine all ingredients, except potatoes and crushed cereal. Blend well and fold in potatoes. Bake in casserole dish at 350° for 40 minutes. Remove and add cereal. Bake 10 minutes until done.

Yield: 10 servings
❦ *Calories: 135*
❦ *Fat: 2.5 grams*

"Balance means

making time

for family,

for spiritual,

personal growth

& for rest. No,

I'm not perfect

& people tell me

I need to listen to

what I preach.

I'm always

striving to

do better."

MAIN DISHES

"Guiltless Family Favorites"

Working Woman's Low Fat Chicken and Dumplings

1 large can fat free chicken broth	4 boneless skinless chicken breasts
5-6 cups water	½ cup fat free margarine
1 tablespoon onion powder	1 cup reduced fat cream of chicken soup
1 teaspoon garlic powder	20 fat free flour tortillas
salt and pepper to taste	
½ cup chopped celery	

In a large saucepan, combine chicken broth, water, seasonings, and celery. Bring to a boil. Place chicken in boiling mixture and cook until tender. After chicken is completely cooked, remove and cut into small pieces. Set aside. Add margarine and cream of chicken soup to boiling water; bring to a boil. Cut tortillas into strips and add to boiling broth mixture. Cook about 10-15 minutes or until tender. Add chicken. If mixture is too thick, add skim milk.

Yield: 16 servings
❦ *Calories: 125*
❦ *Fat: 1.5 grams*

Reduced Fat Southwest Chicken Casserole

½ cup green bell pepper, chopped
½ cup onion, chopped
½ cup chicken broth
4 cups crushed low fat baked tortilla chips
2 cups cooked chicken, chopped
⅓ cup minced fresh cilantro (optional)
1 (15¼-ounce) can golden sweet whole kernel corn, drained
1 (14½-ounce) can Mexican-style stewed tomatoes, undrained
8 ounces fat free sour cream
1½ teaspoons ground cumin
1 cup (4 ounces) shredded Mexican cheese blend, divided

Sauté peppers and onion in chicken broth until tender. Add remaining ingredients and stir in ½ cup cheese. Spread mixture in a lightly greased 2-quart shallow baking dish. Bake, covered, at 375° for 30 minutes. Uncover; sprinkle with remaining cheese. Bake 5 more minutes or until cheese melts.

Yield: 8 servings
❦ *Calories: 270*
❦ *Fat: 6½ grams*

Reduced Fat Poppy Seed Chicken Casserole

2 packages reduced fat Ritz crackers, crushed
3 tablespoons poppy seeds
almonds, chopped (optional)
½ cup reduced fat margarine, melted
4 chicken breasts, boiled and cubed

1 can reduced fat cream of mushroom soup
1 can reduced fat cream of celery soup
8 ounces light sour cream
celery, garlic powder, onion, salt and pepper to taste

Mix crackers, poppy seeds and melted margarine, reserving some for topping. Cover bottom of baking dish. Combine other ingredients. Spread over cracker layer. Top with remaining cracker mixture. Bake at 350° for 30 minutes.

Yield: 18 servings of ½ cup each
❦ *Calories: 145*
❦ *Fat: 5½ grams*

Reduced Fat Mexican Chicken & Dressing

For extra Mexican flavor, add jalapeno peppers and a small jar of red pimentos.

3 (5-ounce) boneless skinless chicken breasts	1 onion, chopped
6 boiled eggs (omit yolks), chopped	1 (6-ounce) package Mexican cornbread mix
1 can reduced fat cream of chicken soup	1 (6-ounce) package yellow cornbread mix
1 can reduced fat cream of celery soup	salt and pepper to taste

In large saucepan, boil chicken and reserve broth. Chop cooked chicken; then return to saucepan and add eggs, soups and onion. Bake cornbread mixes according to package directions. Crumble cornbread and add to other ingredients. Stir in enough chicken broth to make soupy consistency. Salt and pepper to taste. Pour ingredients in casserole dish and bake at 350° for about 45 minutes to desired consistency.

Yield: 16 servings
❦ *Calories: 180*
❦ *Fat: 5 grams*

Reduced Fat Mamaw's Chicken Rice Bake

1 can reduced fat cream of mushroom soup	1 (10-ounce) package frozen peas and carrots, thawed
1 cup skim milk	
1 envelope onion mix	4-6 small skinless soup chicken breasts, boiled
1 small can sliced or chopped mushrooms	
1 cup white or brown rice	paprika

In a mixing bowl stir together soup, milk, dry soup mix, and undrained mushrooms. Reserve ½ cup soup mixture and set aside. Stir uncooked rice and thawed vegetables into remaining soup mixture. Pour into baking dish; arrange boiled chicken breasts on top. Pour reserved soup mixture over chicken. Sprinkle chicken with paprika. Cover with lid or aluminum foil. Bake at 375° until rice is tender, about 1½ hours for regular rice. May reduce cooking time by using instant rice.

Yield: 8 servings.
❦ *Calories: 275*
❦ *Fat: 3 grams*

Reduced Fat King Ranch Chicken

1 pound light Velveeta cheese, cubed
1 (10-ounce) can Rotel diced tomatoes and green chilies
2 large chicken breasts, cooked, or 2 (10-ounce) cans chunk white chicken, shredded
1 (10¾-ounce) can reduced fat cream of mushroom soup
1 can reduced fat cream of chicken soup
1 (7½-ounce) bag WOW Reduced Fat Doritos chips

Melt Velveeta in microwave with Rotel; set aside. Preheat oven to 350°. Spray 9 × 13-inch casserole dish with nonstick cooking spray. In separate bowl, mix cooked chicken and soups; set aside. Line casserole dish with layer of chips; add chicken mixture. Pour Rotel over chicken and continue layering ingredients, finishing with cheese as top layer. Bake at 350° for 30 minutes.

Yield: 12 servings
❦ *Calories: 220*
❦ *Fat: 8 grams*

Reduced Fat Fettuccine Alfredo

Every bit as good as the original!
Serve over whole wheat fettuccine pasta.

1   onion, chopped
1   green bell pepper, chopped
2-3 stalks celery, chopped
½   cup green onions, chopped
1   cup mushrooms, sliced
½   pound boneless skinless chicken breasts, cooked and sliced
8   ounces light Velveeta cheese
½   cup chicken broth
1   cup fat free evaporated skim milk
¾   cup grated Parmesan cheese

Sauté vegetables in skillet with nonstick cooking spray until slightly tender. Add chicken. In microwave, melt Velveeta with chicken broth and add to skillet. Stir in skim milk and Parmesan cheese. Simmer sauce over low heat until serving.

Yield: 8 servings
❧ *Calories: 190*
❧ *Fat: 7 grams*

Reduced Fat Chicken-Almond Casserole

2 cups chicken breast, cooked and chopped
1 can reduced fat cream of mushroom soup
1 can cheddar cheese soup
2 cups 99% fat free chicken broth
2 cups cooked rice
1 (7-ounce) can chopped green chilies, drained
1 (4-ounce) can chopped pimentos, drained
minced onion to taste
¼ cup sliced almonds
8 slices fat free sharp cheddar cheese

Preheat oven to 350°. Combine chicken, soups, broth, rice, chilies, pimentos, and minced onion in a large bowl; mix well. Pour into a prepared 9 × 13-inch casserole dish. Top with cheese and almonds. Bake until heated through and cheese melts.

Yield: 12 servings
❦ *Calories: 150*
❦ *Fat: 4 grams*

Reduced Fat Chicken Roll-Ups

3 (4-ounce) boneless skinless chicken breasts, seasoned and cooked
1 can reduced fat crescent rolls
1 cup reduced fat shredded cheese
1 can reduced fat cream of mushroom soup
1 can reduced fat cream of chicken soup

Cube or shred cooked chicken and combine with cheddar cheese. Open crescent roll triangles and distribute chicken mixture evenly on each roll. Roll up and place rolls in casserole dish sprayed with nonstick cooking spray. Mix soups together and pour over crescent rolls. Bake at 350° until bubbly.

Yield 8 servings
❦ *Calories: 270*
❦ *Fat: 10 grams*

Reduced Fat Cheesy Chicken Spectacular

3 boneless skinless chicken breasts (or enough for 3 cups diced)
1 (12-ounce) package long grain and wild rice combination or 1 package brown rice
1 medium onion, finely chopped
1 pound light Velveeta cheese
1 (10¾-ounce) can reduced fat cream of celery soup
1 (6- or 8-ounce) jar canned sliced mushrooms, drained
1 (10-ounce) can diced Rotel tomatoes, drained
1 (16-ounce) can French cut green beans, drained
salt and pepper to taste
shredded cheddar cheese for garnish

Boil chicken and dice coarsely. Cook rice in chicken stock. In large boiler, sauté onions and melt cheese. Lightly combine all ingredients. Place in 1 large or 2 medium casseroles. Garnish with cheese and bake at 350° for about 30 minutes or until lightly browned.

Yield: 10 servings of about 1 cup each
❦ *Calories: 325*
❦ *Fat: 7½ grams*

Reduced Fat Almond Chicken Stir-Fry

1 tablespoon cooking sherry	1 small can bamboo shoots
1 tablespoon water	1 small can water chestnuts, sliced thin
1 tablespoon soy sauce	
1 tablespoon cornstarch	1 cup fresh mushrooms, sliced or 1 small can, sliced
1 pound boneless skinless chicken breasts, sliced into thin strips	
	½ cup frozen peas
1 tablespoon olive oil	⅓ cup slivered almonds

Combine cooking sherry, water, soy sauce, and cornstarch. Marinate chicken in mixture. In a nonstick skillet sprayed with cooking spray, sauté vegetables and almonds in oil, stirring constantly. Remove from pan and set aside. Sauté chicken in skillet with marinade mixture, stirring quickly, until meat turns white. Add more water, sherry, and soy sauce if pan boils dry. When chicken is almost done, return vegetables to pan. Push meat and vegetables to side of skillet and add cornstarch to liquid until thick and the consistency of gravy. Serve over rice.

Yield: 8 servings
❦ *Calories: 200*
❦ *Fat: 5 grams*

Mom's Day Out Crock Pot Chicken Casserole

Any day is a good day to celebrate Mother's Day. This slow cooker recipe is so easy that the kids and Dad can assemble it, and surprise Mom with a great dinner made just for her!

1 (8-ounce) package noodles, any variety
3 cups diced cooked chicken
1½ cups frozen vegetable blend (onion, bell pepper, celery)
1 (4-ounce) can sliced mushrooms, drained
1 (4-ounce) jar pimiento, diced
½ cup fat free grated Parmesan cheese
1½ cups reduced fat cream-style cottage cheese
1 cup shredded reduced fat sharp cheddar cheese
1 can reduced fat cream of chicken soup
½ cup chicken broth
2 tablespoons reduced fat margarine
1 teaspoon Italian seasoning

Cook noodles according to package directions in boiling water until barely tender; drain and rinse thoroughly. In a large bowl, combine remaining ingredients with noodles, making certain the noodles are separated and coated with liquid. Pour mixture into slow cooker sprayed with nonstick spray. Cover and cook on low setting for 6-10 hours, or on high setting for 3-4 hours.

Yield: 12 servings.
❦ *Calories: 215*
❦ *Fat: 5 grams*

Low Fat White Chicken Chili

2½ cups chicken broth
1   teaspoon ground
    cumin
2   teaspoons lemon
    pepper
4   boneless skinless
    chicken breasts
2-3 tablespoons
    minced garlic
1   cup onion, chopped

2   (4-ounce) cans
    green chilies
3   tablespoons lime
    juice
1   (15-ounce) can
    whole kernel white
    corn, drained
2   (14-ounce) cans
    white Great
    Northern beans

Boil chicken in broth, cumin and lemon pepper; cut into bite size pieces. Add garlic and onion, reduce heat to low and allow to simmer until tender. Add remaining ingredients, except beans, and bring to a boil. Reduce heat and add beans; simmer until thoroughly heated, about 30 minutes. May be served over low fat crushed tortilla chips and low fat Monterey Jack cheese. Top with low fat sour cream and salsa.

Yield: 10 servings
❦ *Calories: 210*
❦ *Fat: 2 grams*

Reduced Fat Cheesy Squash & Chicken Casserole

1	tablespoon reduced fat margarine	1	cup shredded reduced fat cheddar cheese
1	cup chopped onion	2	cooked chicken breasts, chopped
6	cups sliced or chopped squash	12	reduced fat Ritz crackers, crumbled
1	can reduced fat cream of chicken soup	2	tablespoons reduced fat margarine, melted
8	ounces light sour cream		

Preheat oven to 350°. Melt 1 tablespoon margarine in large skillet over medium to high heat; add onion and squash. Spray with nonstick cooking spray as needed. To maintain a good combination of texture, sauté 3-4 cups squash and gradually add remaining. After squash are tender; add soup, sour cream, ½ cup cheese, and chicken. Stir over low heat until well blended. Pour mixture into casserole dish prepared with nonstick cooking spray. In separate bowl, combine crackers, ½ cup cheese, and melted margarine; sprinkle cracker mixture on top of casserole. Bake 8-10 minutes until bubbly.

Yield: 12 servings.
❦ *Calories: 155*
❦ *Fat: 6 grams*

Low Fat Mexican Casserole

1   pound boneless
    skinless chicken
    breasts, cooked
    and cubed
2   cups crushed baked
    low fat tortilla chips
1   can Rotel diced
    tomatoes
1   cup salsa
1   small onion, chopped

1   can reduced fat cream
    of mushroom soup
1   can reduced fat cream
    of chicken soup
10 slices fat free sharp
    cheddar cheese
¼   cup shredded
    reduced fat cheddar
    cheese

Cover the bottom of a large casserole dish with crushed chips. Add chicken. In separate bowl, combine Rotel tomatoes, salsa and onion. Pour tomato mixture over chips and chicken. Combine soups and pour over tomato mixture. Top with cheeses. Cook at 375° for 15 minutes or until cheese melts.

Yield: 8 servings
❦ *Calories: 235*
❦ *Fat: 4½ grams*

Low Fat Chicken Rolls

These easy rolls may be frozen. Before baking, place chicken rolls on cookie sheet and freeze until firm. Remove and store in zip bags in freezer until ready to bake.

4   chicken breasts, boiled and finely chopped
green onions, chopped
8   ounces fat free cream cheese
Tony Chachere's Original Seasoning

2   cans reduced fat crescent rolls
fat free liquid margarine
seasoned bread crumbs

Combine first four ingredients. Open crescent rolls into triangles. Spoon chicken mixture onto middle of each roll and wrap up, overlapping sides. Roll in fat free margarine; then in seasoned bread crumbs. Place rolls on cookie sheet and bake at 425° for about 10-15 minutes.

Yield: 16 rolls
❦ *Calories: 190*
❦ *Fat: 5½ grams*

Low Fat Chicken Ole' Casserole

2 cups chicken, cooked and diced
4 cups wide noodles, cooked
¼ cup onion, chopped
1 (4-ounce) can green chilies, chopped
1 (10¾-ounce) can reduced fat cream of chicken soup

½-¾ cup chicken broth
½ cup light sour cream
1 teaspoon salt
½ teaspoon pepper
1 cup grated reduced fat cheddar cheese
6 slices fat free sharp cheddar cheese
freshly grated Parmesan cheese, if desired

Mix all ingredients together with 1 cup grated cheddar. (Use ½ cup chicken broth at first, adding more to reach desired consistency.) Pour into greased 2-quart casserole dish. Place slices of sharp cheddar on top. For extra flavor, sprinkle with freshly grated Parmesan cheese. Bake at 350° for 45 minutes to 1 hour.

Yield: 10 servings of ¾ cup each
❦ *Calories: 260*
❦ *Fat: 5 grams*

Busy Mom's Low Fat Chicken Pot Pie

You may substitute your choice of vegetables for the sweet peas (i.e. diced carrots).

1 pound boneless skinless chicken breasts
1 can fat free chicken broth
2 teaspoons dry ButterBuds
celery salt, onion powder, salt and pepper to taste

1 cup sweet peas with pearl onions
1 can reduced fat cream of chicken soup
1 can reduced fat cream of mushroom soup
1 can low fat biscuits

Boil chicken breasts in chicken broth. Add dry Butter Buds and seasonings to taste. Remove chicken from broth and cut into bite-sized pieces. In casserole dish, combine 1 cup chicken broth, chicken, peas, and soups. Mix all ingredients well; top with biscuits. Bake at 375° for 20-30 minutes or until biscuits are cooked completely and casserole is bubbly.

Yield: 10 servings with one biscuit each
❦ *Calories: 165*
❦ *Fat: 3 grams*

Best Ever Low Fat Baked Chicken

*You'll vote for this chicken over
fried chicken anytime!*

½ cup bread crumbs
¼ cup fat free
    Parmesan cheese
1 teaspoon rosemary
1 teaspoon basil
½ teaspoon oregano
1 teaspoon black
    pepper

1 tablespoon parsley
    flakes
4 boneless skinless
    chicken breasts
½ cup liquid fat free
    margarine

Combine bread crumbs, cheese, and seasoning in a shallow bowl. Dip each chicken breast in liquid margarine; then in bread crumb mixture. Place chicken breasts on baking sheet sprayed with nonstick cooking spray. Bake at 375° for about 30-45 minutes or until golden brown.

Yield: 4 servings
❦ *Calories: 230*
❦ *Fat: 4.5 grams*

Low Fat
Chicken Lagnaippe

For faster preparation, you may substitute
1 (10-ounce) package frozen vegetable blend,
which includes onion, bell pepper, and celery.

4 cups chicken, cooked and chopped
1 (16-ounce) package whole wheat spiral noodles
1½ cups celery, chopped
½ cup onion, chopped
⅓ cup green bell pepper
1 tablespoon margarine
2 cans reduced fat cream of mushroom soup

⅔ cups skim milk
½ teaspoon salt
¼ teaspoon Nature's Seasoning
¼ teaspoon white pepper
1 pound light Velveeta cheese, cubed
1 large jar pimento

Boil noodles in chicken broth. Sauté celery, onion and bell pepper in margarine. Mix soup, milk, and seasonings. Add chopped pimento. Combine noodles, chicken, soup mixture and vegetables. Add cheese. Mix all ingredients in large casserole dish. Top with remaining cheese. Bake at 325° until bubbly.

Yield: 18 servings of 1 cup each
❦ *Calories: 185*
❦ *Fat: 5 grams*

Easy Low Fat Chicken Cordon Bleu

4   boneless skinless   ¼   cup white cooking
    chicken breasts   wine
8   slices fat free Swiss   1   cup herb stuffing mix
    cheese   salt and pepper to taste
1   can reduced fat
    cream of chicken
    soup

Pat chicken dry and lay pieces in casserole dish. Place two slices of cheese on each chicken breast. In separate bowl, mix soup and wine together. Pour mixture over chicken. Sprinkle stuffing mix on top. Bake at 350° for 40-45 minutes.

Yield: 4 servings
❦ *Calories: 310*
❦ *Fat: 6 grams*

Low Fat Cheesy Chicken and Spaghetti

This is a great recipe to take to a friend.
It is my family's favorite!

1   pound boneless skinless chicken breasts
1   (16-ounce) package spaghetti noodles
1   can fat free chicken broth
1   onion, chopped
1   green bell pepper, chopped
3-4 stalks celery, chopped
fat free margarine
1   pound reduced fat Velveeta cheese, cut up
2   cans Rotel tomatoes, diced
1   can reduced fat cream of chicken soup
1   can reduced fat cream of mushroom soup
1   large can sweet peas

Boil chicken with chicken broth; salt and pepper to taste. Cool and pull meat apart. Cook spaghetti in chicken broth. Sauté onions, bell peppers, and celery in small amount of broth and fat free margarine. Add to spaghetti and stir in chicken, cheese, and Rotel tomatoes. Stir over low heat until cheese melts. Add peas with juice, and soups. Place in large casserole dish and bake at 350° for about 20 minutes.

Yield: 16 servings
❦ *Calories: 270*
❦ *Fat: 5 grams*

Low Fat Chicken Stuffed Shells

For variety, omit pasta shells. Place chicken mixture in casserole dish; top with crushed reduced fat Ritz crackers for a wonderful quick and easy low fat chicken casserole.

24 jumbo pasta shells, cooked
3 boneless skinless chicken breasts
salt and pepper
1 cup fat free sour cream
2 cans reduced fat cream of chicken soup
½ teaspoon pepper
½ teaspoon celery powder or celery salt
2 tablespoons reduced fat margarine, melted
¼ cup seasoned bread crumbs

Boil chicken, adding salt and pepper to taste. Allow to cool; cut into bite size pieces. Combine chicken, sour cream, soup, and seasonings in mixing bowl, stirring well. Place approximately 1 tablespoon chicken mixture in each cooked and cooled pasta shell. Place 1 teaspoon bread crumbs on each stuffed shell; drizzle with melted margarine. Place shells in casserole dish, sprayed lightly with nonstick cooking spray. Bake covered at 350° for 25 minutes.

Yield: 24 servings
❦ *Calories: 85*
❦ *Fat: 2 grams*

Low Fat Mexican Pasta

2 boneless skinless chicken breasts (about 3 ounces each)
fajita seasoning
4 cups spiral pasta, cooked and drained
½ cup light Velveeta cheese, melted

¼ cup Rotel tomatoes, chopped
½ cup enchilada sauce
4 corn tortillas, toasted and shredded
2 cups shredded fat free cheddar cheese

Garnish:

fat free sour cream
sliced jalapeno peppers

sliced green onions

Cook chicken with seasoning in nonstick skillet until brown; cube. To make four individual servings, place 1 cup pasta in each of 4 medium bowls. Add ¼ of the cubed chicken breast to each bowl. Mix melted Velveeta, tomatoes, and enchilada sauce and pour over chicken in each bowl, distributing evenly. Shred one toasted corn tortilla over cheese mixture. Sprinkle ½ cup cheddar cheese over each tortilla. Garnish each serving with 1 tablespoon fat free sour cream, chopped jalapeno peppers, and green onions.

Yield: 4 individual servings
❦ *Calories: 375*
❦ *Fat: 5 grams*

Reduced Fat Chicken Enchilada Pasta

1 cup onion, chopped
1 cup green bell pepper, chopped
1 cup celery, chopped
2 cups yellow squash, cubed
2 cups zucchini squash, cubed
2 large boneless skinless chicken breasts, cooked and chopped

1 (19-ounce) can enchilada sauce
1 (14½-ounce) can diced tomatoes, drained
8 ounces cooked pasta (5-6 cups)
2/3 cup Mexican cheese blend

Sauté onion, bell pepper, and celery in skillet sprayed with nonstick cooking spray. Add squash and continue cooking until squash is tender. Add remaining ingredients. Transfer into large casserole dish and top with shredded cheese. Bake at 350° for 15 minutes or until cheese melts.

Yield: 14 servings of 1 cup each
❦ *Calories: 165*
❦ *Fat: 4 grams*

Peach Glazed Cornish Hens

*Here is another way to enjoy
those sweet Ruston peaches! The glaze is also
delicious on chicken breasts.*

8   Cornish hens
salt and pepper to taste
onion powder to taste

cayenne pepper to taste
thyme, basil and
    tarragon to taste

Glaze:

12 ounces Ruston
    peach preserves

juice of one lemon
¼ cup Kitchen Bouquet

Season Cornish hens to taste. Wrap with foil and bake for 1 hour. Uncover hens and baste with glaze; bake for 15 minutes.

Yield: 8 servings
❦ *Calories: 220*
❦ *Fat: 12 grams*

Orange Marmalade Cornish Hens

Remove skin from Cornish hens to significantly reduce fat grams. This sauce is delicious on boneless, skinless chicken breasts!

8   Cornish hens
salt and pepper
8   onions
½   cup reduced fat margarine
¼   cup Kitchen Bouquet
1   (8-ounce) jar orange marmalade
salt and pepper

Clean and dry hens. Salt and pepper inside and out. Insert an onion in the cavity of each hen. In small saucepan, combine remaining ingredients, heating until margarine melts. Brush sauce over hens. Bake in covered roasting pan at 350° about 1½ hours, removing cover for final 10-15 minutes.

Yield: 8 servings
❦ *Calories: 240*
❦ *Fat: 14 grams*

Reduced Fat Chili Casserole

1 small onion, chopped
2 teaspoons minced garlic
1 tablespoon reduced fat margarine
2 (15-ounce) cans 99% fat free turkey chili (no beans)
1 (16-ounce) jar salsa
½ cup fat free Egg Beaters
1 (12-ounce) container fat free cottage cheese
1 cup shredded reduced fat sharp cheddar cheese
10 egg roll wraps
6 slices fat free sharp cheddar cheese

Sauté onion and garlic in margarine in a large skillet over medium-high heat until tender. Stir in chili and salsa; cook until thoroughly heated. Spoon ½ mixture into a lightly greased 13 × 9-inch baking dish. Stir together Egg Beaters, cottage cheese, and 1 cup Cheddar cheese. Spoon about ¼ mixture evenly on 1 side of each egg roll wrap, and roll up. Place in baking dish, seam side down. Spoon remaining chili mixture evenly over top, spreading to completely cover wrappers. Bake, covered, at 350° for 45 minutes. Uncover and place cheddar cheese slices on top. Bake 5 more minutes or until cheese is melted. Let stand 5 minutes before serving.

Yield: 12 servings
❦ *Calories: 195*
❦ *Fat: 3½ grams*

Low Fat Black Eye Cornbread Casserole

½ pound turkey sausage, ground
1 onion, chopped
½ green bell pepper, chopped
1 small package frozen cream style corn or 1 large can
1 package corn bread mix
½ cup fat free Egg Beaters
1 cup low fat buttermilk
1 large can black eye peas, including liquid
4 ounces shredded reduced fat cheddar cheese

Spray large skillet with nonstick cooking spray. Sauté sausage, onion, and bell pepper until tender. Add frozen corn and continue to sauté for about 5 minutes. In large mixing bowl, combine cornbread mix, Egg Beaters, and buttermilk. When cornbread mix is blended, fold in peas, cheese, and sausage mixture. Bake at 350° for 1 hour in 9 × 13-inch casserole dish.

Yield: 16 servings
❦ *Calories: 140*
❦ *Fat: 4.5 grams*

Reduced Fat Mexican Lasagna

1	pound ground turkey or lean ground beef	1	can Rotel tomatoes, diced
2	teaspoons ground cumin	10	corn tortillas
1	tablespoon chili powder	1	cup fat free small curd cottage cheese
1	tablespoon Season All	1	cup fat free sour cream
1	teaspoon black pepper	1	cup shredded fat free cheddar cheese
½	teaspoon garlic powder	2	egg whites

Top Layer:

2	cups shredded lettuce	½	cup shredded fat free cheddar cheese
1	cup chopped tomatoes		
3	green onions, chopped		

Brown ground turkey or beef in nonstick skillet. Add all seasonings and Rotel tomatoes and heat through. Cover bottom of a rectangle glass baking dish with 5 corn tortillas. Pour turkey mixture over tortillas; place the other 5 tortillas over meat mixture. Combine cottage cheese, sour cream, 1 cup cheddar cheese and egg whites in mixing bowl. Blend mixture together thoroughly and pour over tortillas. Bake at 350° for 30 minutes. Remove from oven. Before serving, garnish with top layer ingredients. Sprinkle lettuce diagonally across center, cheddar cheese on each side of lettuce, and tomatoes on each side of cheddar cheese. Sprinkle green onions on each side of tomatoes.

Yield: 8 servings
❦ *Calories: 368*
❦ *Fat: 8 grams*

Reduced Fat
Tater Tot Casserole

1½ pounds lean
    ground beef
1 cup frozen vegetable
    blend (onion, bell
    pepper, celery)
36 frozen tater tots

1 cup skim milk
1 can reduced fat
    cream of mushroom
    soup
1 cup shredded fat
    free cheddar cheese

Sauté meat with vegetables; pour into 9 × 13-inch casserole dish. Spread tater tots evenly over meat mixture. Combine milk and soup and pour evenly over tater tots. Top with cheese and bake at 350° for about 30 minutes until bubbly.

Yield: 12 servings
❦ *Calories: 175*
❦ *Fat: 7 grams*

Low Fat Hot Tamale Pie

This pie is even better when refrigerated several hours or overnight before baking!

2   cups crushed baked low fat corn chips
½   cup Egg Beaters or 1 egg
1   pound lean ground beef
½   cup chopped green bell pepper
1   (16-ounce) can fat free spicy refried beans
1   (10-ounce) can Rotel tomatoes
½   (10-ounce) can enchilada sauce
taco seasoning to taste
onion and garlic powder to taste
½   cup shredded fat free cheddar cheese

Spray casserole dish with nonstick cooking spray. Mix corn chips and Egg Beaters and press evenly into casserole dish. Cook lean beef in large saucepan until brown. Sauté chopped bell pepper. Stir in beans, tomatoes, enchilada sauce and all seasonings. Spoon mixture over crust and sprinkle with cheese. Bake uncovered at 350-375° for 25-30 minutes.

Yield: 12 servings
❦ *Calories: 215*
❦ *Fat: 3 grams*

Low Fat Baked Cabbage Jambalaya

½ pound lean ground meat

Louisiana seasonings to taste (Tony Chachere's Original Seasoning, garlic powder, etc.)

1 onion, chopped

1 pound low fat smoked sausage, cut into pieces

1 head cabbage, chopped or 1 package shredded cabbage (about ¾ of a 1-pound package)

1 cup raw brown rice, washed

chili powder to taste

⅓ cup chicken broth

½ teaspoon Tabasco Pepper Sauce

1 can Rotel tomatoes

Sauté ground meat and season to taste. Add chopped onion and smoked sausage; cook until onions are clear. Add all other ingredients and pour into a casserole dish. Cover and bake at 275° for 2 hours, stirring halfway through cooking time.

Yield: 16 servings
❦ *Calories: 130*
❦ *Fat: 3 grams*

Reduced Fat Slow Cooker Lasagna

1 pound ground round	9 lasagna noodles, uncooked
1 teaspoon dried Italian seasoning	1 jar sliced mushrooms
1 (28-ounce) jar spaghetti sauce	1 (15-ounce) carton fat free ricotta cheese
⅓ cup water	1 cup fat free shredded mozzarella cheese

Cook beef with Italian seasoning in large skillet over medium-high heat, stirring until beef crumbles. Drain. Combine spaghetti sauce and water in a small bowl. Place 4 uncooked noodles in bottom of a lightly greased 5-quart electric slow cooker. Layer with half each of beef mixture, spaghetti sauce mixture, and mushrooms. Spread ricotta cheese over mushrooms. Sprinkle with ½ cup mozzarella cheese. Layer with the remaining noodles, meat, sauce mixture, mushrooms, and mozzarella cheese. Cover and cook on high setting 1 hour; reduce heat and cook on low setting 5 hours.

Yield: 12 servings
❦ *Calories: 130*
❦ *Fat: 5 grams*

Reduced Fat Meat and Cheese Pistolettes

This hearty filling is also great as a dip!

1 pound lean ground beef, browned
1 medium onion, diced
1 can diced Rotel tomatoes
8 ounces light sour cream
1 can reduced fat cream of chicken soup
1 can reduced fat cream of mushroom soup
32 pistolette rolls

Combine ingredients and fill each roll with ⅓ cup mixture. Cover and heat at 350° for 10 minutes.

Yield: 32 servings
❦ *Calories: 125*
❦ *Fat: 4½ grams*

Reduced Fat Pizza Pie

¾ pound lean ground beef

½ cup frozen vegetable blend (onion, bell pepper, celery)

1 (14-ounce) jar spaghetti sauce or ½ of a large jar

1 cup shredded reduced fat mozzarella cheese

1 (8-count) can reduced fat crescent rolls

grated Parmesan cheese

Preheat oven to 350°. Brown ground beef with vegetables in nonstick skillet. Stir until crumbly; drain. Stir in spaghetti sauce. Simmer for 5 minutes. Spread mixture into 11 × 13-inch baking pan. Sprinkle with mozzarella cheese. Unroll crescent dough and lay over top of pie, sealing perforations. Sprinkle with Parmesan cheese. Bake 8-10 minutes or until golden brown.

Yield: 8 servings
❦ *Calories: 205*
❦ *Fat: 5 grams*

Reduced Fat Crescent Pizza Pie

1 pound lean ground beef	¼ teaspoon pepper
¼ cup chopped onion	1 (4-ounce) can chopped mushrooms
¼ cup chopped green bell pepper	1 (8-ounce) can refrigerated crescent rolls
1 (15-ounce) can tomato sauce	½ cup fat free Egg Beaters plus one egg white
1 teaspoon parsley flakes	
½ teaspoon leaf oregano	8 slices fat free mozzarella cheese
1 teaspoon leaf basil	1 tablespoon water
¼ teaspoon salt	

Brown the ground beef, onion, and bell pepper until onion is clear; drain fat. Stir in tomato sauce, parsley, oregano, basil, salt, pepper, and mushrooms. Set aside. Unroll crescent rolls into triangles. In lightly greased pie plate, press 4 triangles together to form crust. Beat ½ cup Egg Beaters and pour *half* over pie shell. Spoon meat mixture into shell; arrange cheese slices on top. Spread with remaining Egg Beaters. Mix egg white with water and set aside. Place remaining four sections of dough together to form top crust. Brush with egg white and water mixture. Trim; seal and flute edges. Slit top crust. Bake at 350° about 25 minutes or until golden brown.

Yield: 8 servings
❦ *Calories: 225*
❦ *Fat: 5 grams*

Reduced Fat Chuck Wagon Chili Casserole

1 pound lean ground beef	¾ cup barbecue sauce
½ cup onion, chopped	1 (8½-ounce) package corn muffin mix
½ cup green bell pepper, chopped	1 (11-ounce) can Mexican-style corn, drained
1 (15½-ounce) can mild chili beans in sauce	

Preheat oven to 400°. In frying pan, cook and stir ground beef, onion, and bell pepper over medium heat about 8-10 minutes or until beef is no longer pink. Drain. Stir in chili beans and barbecue sauce. Bring to a boil. Spoon mixture into a 9-inch casserole dish. In separate bowl, prepare corn muffin mix according to package directions, using skim milk. Stir in corn. Spoon over meat mixture. Bake 30 minutes or until golden brown.

Yield: 8 servings
❦ *Calories: 300*
❦ *Fat: 8 grams*

Reduced Fat Chili Spaghetti

Remember that you may substitute whole wheat pasta in pasta recipes!

1½ pounds lean ground beef
1 (46-ounce) can tomato juice
1 (15-ounce) can tomato sauce
1 large onion, chopped
1 large green bell pepper, chopped

2 bay leaves
chili powder to taste
salt to taste
parsley flakes to taste
pepper to taste
2 (15-ounce) cans pinto beans
small package spaghetti

Brown ground beef and drain. Add all other ingredients, except pinto beans and spaghetti. Bring to a boil; then simmer 2 hours over low heat. Add beans and simmer another 30-40 minutes, adding water as needed. Add spaghetti and cook until noodles are done.

Yield: 16 servings
❦ *Calories: 195*
❦ *Fat: 4 grams*

Reduced Fat Chili Bake

One cup of my Reduced Fat Chili Bake and a large green salad is a great meal for less than 400 calories. This is also a good recipe for using ground venison or elk. Regular ground beef can increase fat to more than 20 grams per serving.

1	pound lean ground beef or turkey	⅓	cup chili seasoning
1	(15-ounce) can pinto beans, drained	1	cup (4 ounces) shredded sharp reduced fat American cheese
1	(10-ounce) can hot enchilada sauce	4	ounces baked tortilla chips
1	(8-ounce) can tomato sauce		

Garnish:

1	cup light sour cream	½	cup (2 ounces) shredded sharp American cheese

Brown ground beef in skillet. Stir in drained beans, enchilada sauce, tomato sauce, chili seasoning and shredded cheese. Coarsely crush chips and stir into meat mixture. Turn into a 1½-quart casserole. Bake, covered, at 375° for 30 minutes. Spoon sour cream over casserole; sprinkle with cheese. Sprinkle reserved chips around edge of casserole. Bake, uncovered, 2 to 3 minutes.

Yield: 7 servings of one cup each
❦ *Calories: 360 (without garnish)*
❦ *Fat: 12 grams*

Reduced Fat Cabbage Roll Casserole

1 medium head cabbage, chopped	1 can water
¾ pound lean ground beef or ground turkey	1 teaspoon granulated sugar or sugar substitute
1 onion, chopped	4 heaping tablespoons raw rice
⅓ cup chopped green onion	½ teaspoon paprika
½ cup chopped green bell pepper	¼ teaspoon red pepper
2 small cans tomato sauce	salt and pepper to taste

Brown meat and onion; add green onion and bell pepper. Drain. Mix tomato sauce, water, sugar, and rice. Spray 9 × 12-inch casserole dish with nonstick cooking spray and place layer of cabbage (about 1½-inch thick). Sprinkle paprika, salt and pepper over cabbage. Spread meat mixture in a layer over cabbage. Pour soup mixture on top; cover with aluminum foil and bake at 325° for 45 minutes to one hour.

Yield: 6 servings
❦ *Calories: 220*
❦ *Fat: 4½ grams*

Reduced Fat Beef & Salsa Burritos

1¼ pounds lean
    ground beef
1½ tablespoons chili
    powder
½ teaspoon ground
    cumin
½ teaspoon salt
¼ teaspoon pepper
1 (10-ounce) package
    frozen chopped
    spinach, thawed
    and well drained

1¼ cups prepared
    chunky salsa
½ cup shredded fat
    free cheddar cheese
½ cup shredded
    cheddar cheese
10 medium low fat
    flour tortillas,
    warmed

In large nonstick skillet, brown ground beef over medium heat 10-12 minutes or until no longer pink, stirring occasionally. Drain. Season beef with chili powder, cumin, salt and pepper. Stir in spinach and salsa; heat through. Remove from heat; stir in cheese. Spoon ½ cup beef mixture on center of each tortilla. Fold bottom edge up over filling; fold sides to center, overlapping edges.

Yield: 10 servings
❦ *Calories: 200*
❦ *Fat: 6 grams*

Low Fat Speedy Taco Bake

1	pound lean ground beef	6	slices fat free cheese
½	cup chopped onion	1	cup shredded fat free cheddar cheese
1	envelope (1¼ ounces) taco seasoning mix	½	cup Rotel tomatoes, chopped and drained
1	(15-ounce) can tomato sauce	2	cups regular or reduced fat biscuit and baking mix
1	(15¼-ounce) can whole kernel corn, drained	1	cup skim milk
		2	eggs

Preheat oven to 350°. Brown ground beef and onion; drain. Spoon into ungreased 9 × 13-inch baking dish. Stir in taco seasoning mix (dry), tomato sauce, Rotel tomatoes, and corn. Arrange slices of cheese over mixture and sprinkle with shredded cheese. Mix remaining ingredients until blended and pour over beef mixture. Bake 35 minutes until light golden brown. Serve with sour cream, chopped tomato and shredded lettuce if desired.

Yield: 8 servings of about 1 cup each
❦ *Calories: 375*
❦ *Fat: 5 grams*

Low Fat Lasagna

1 pound lean ground beef	½ cup fat free Egg Beaters
¾ cup chopped onion	½ cup grated fat free Parmesan cheese
1 (16-ounce) can diced tomatoes	8 ounces lasagna noodles
1 (12-ounce) can tomato paste	3 cups shredded fat free mozzarella cheese (reserve ¼ cup for topping)
2 teaspoons basil	
1 teaspoon oregano	
2 teaspoons salt	
3 cups fat free cottage cheese	¼ cup shredded reduced fat cheddar cheese
1 tablespoon parsley flakes	

In skillet, combine beef and onion; cook until brown. Add tomatoes, tomato paste, basil, oregano and salt. Simmer uncovered 30 minutes, stirring occasionally. In separate bowl, combine remaining ingredients except cheddar cheese. Reserve ¼ cup mozzarella for topping. Prepare lasagna noodles according to package; drain. Spray large casserole dish with nonstick cooking spray. Dividing evenly, layer noodles, meat sauce, and cheese mixture. Repeat layers. Sprinkle with ¼ cup mozzarella and cheddar cheese. Bake at 350° for 30 minutes.

Yield: 16 servings
❦ *Calories: 225*
❦ *Fat: 3 grams*

Beef Noodle Casserole

1 pound ground round or extra lean ground beef
½ cup chopped onions
garlic
¼ teaspoon oregano
1 can reduced fat cream of mushroom soup

1 can Rotel tomatoes, chopped
1 (5-ounce) package No-Yolk Egg Noodles, cooked according to directions

Brown meat, onions, garlic, and oregano in nonstick skillet. Add undiluted soup and tomatoes. Combine with cooked noodles and mix well.

Yield: 10 servings
❦ *Calories: 230*
❦ *Fat: 5 grams*

Low Fat Oven Stew

Instead of baking, this stew may cooked in a slow cooker, or boiled on the stovetop until tender.

1½ pound lean stew meat, trimmed of fat
1 large can (15 ounces) beef broth
4 stalks celery, sliced into 1-inch pieces
5 carrots, cleaned and sliced into 1-inch pieces
3 medium onions, sliced in chunks
6 medium potatoes, washed, peeled and cut into chunks
2 small cans tomato paste
2 (15-ounce) cans tomato sauce
3 bay leaves
salt and pepper

Boil stew meat in beef broth. Place meat and broth in large cast iron Dutch oven; add vegetables. Stir in tomato paste, tomato sauce, bay leaves and salt and pepper to taste. Bake at 300° for 3½-4 hours. Stir occasionally and add additional broth or water if needed.

Yield: 22 servings of 1 cup each
❧ *Calories: 130*
❧ *Fat: 3 grams*

Light Filet Mignon

4   ounces lean filet mignon
1   teaspoon chicken soup base

2   small whole potatoes
¾   cup mixed vegetables
½   cup baby carrots

Spray nonstick skillet with cooking spray. Mix 1 teaspoon chicken soup base with 1 cup water. Sauté filet in small amount of soup base on high heat until seared well. Reduce heat to medium and continue cooking until desired doneness. Sauté vegetables in small amount of soup base until tender.

Yield: 1 serving
❦ *Calories: 415*
❦ *Fat: 12 grams*

Beef & Chicken Kabobs

For extra-tender meat, boil pieces in marinade for about 30 minutes.

5   ounces low sodium teriyaki sauce
1   (8-ounce) bottle fat free Italian dressing
¼   cup lemon juice
1   tablespoon garlic powder
salt and pepper to taste
6   ounces lean top sirloin, cubed
6   ounces boneless skinless chicken breast, cubed
2-3 green bell peppers, cubed
2-3 red bell peppers, cubed
2-3 onions, cubed

Mix teriyaki sauce, dressing, lemon juice, garlic powder, salt and pepper in a shallow dish; add cubed meat. Allow meat to marinate overnight. Place meat and vegetables alternately on wood skewer. Place on grill or in nonstick skillet. Cook until tender.

Yield: 4 servings
❣ *Calories: 250*
❣ *Fat: 5½ grams*

Reduced Fat
Pork Chop Casserole

This casserole is delicious made with brown rice!

3-4 lean pork chops
3 cups instant rice
3 cups hot water
1 can reduced fat cream of chicken soup
1 can reduced fat cream of mushroom soup
salt and pepper to taste

Brown pork chops using grill or nonstick skillet without oil; set aside. In casserole dish, mix rice and water; add soups and mix well. Place browned pork chops on top of rice mixture. Cover and bake at 350° for about 30 minutes. Bake uncovered an additional 10-15 minutes.

Yield: 6 servings (1/6 rice mixture plus 1 pork chop)
❦ *Calories: 400*
❦ *Fat: 9 grams*

Low Fat Salmon Croquettes

2   (6-ounce) cans salmon in spring water
¼   cup onion, finely chopped
¾   cup bread crumbs
1   egg, slightly beaten
1   tablespoon lemon juice
¼   teaspoon fresh-ground black pepper
¼   teaspoon nutmeg

Combine all ingredients in a bowl and mix well. Shape into 4 patties approximately ¾-inches thick. Spray a nonstick skillet with cooking spray and fry the patties over moderate heat, turning once, until browned on each side.

Yield: 4 servings
❦ *Calories: 140*
❦ *Fat: 5 grams*

Reduced Fat Tuna Casserole

1 cup macaroni, cooked and drained

1 can reduced fat cream of mushroom soup

1 tablespoon pimento, chopped

1 can solid white tuna, drained

1 tablespoon chopped onion

⅓ cup skim milk

2 tablespoons reduced fat margarine

½ cup fat free saltine crackers, crushed

Stir macaroni, soup, pimento, tuna, onion, and milk together. Place in casserole dish and sprinkle with cracker crumbs. Dot with margarine. Bake at 375° for 20-25 minutes.

Yield: 9 servings
❦ *Calories: 135*
❦ *Fat: 3 grams*

Shrimp Etouffee

salt, black pepper, and
   red pepper to taste
¼ cup margarine
1 package frozen
   vegetable blend
   (onion, bell pepper,
   celery)
¼ teaspoon garlic salt
2 pounds shrimp,
   boiled and peeled

1 (10-ounce) can
   reduced fat cream
   of mushroom soup
1 (10-ounce) can
   reduced fat cream
   of celery soup
1 (10-ounce) can
   tomato soup
hot cooked rice

Season shrimp with salt, black pepper, and red pepper. Melt margarine in nonstick 10-inch skillet. Add frozen vegetable blend and garlic salt. Cook over low heat until onion is wilted. Stir in shrimp. Simmer for 20 minutes. Add soups; mix well. Cook for one minute longer. Serve over hot rice.

Yield: 12 servings of ½ cup each
❦ *Calories: 140*
❦ *Fat: 4 grams*

Reduced Fat Shrimp Delight

This easy dish is great served over rice!

1 onion, chopped	1 can cream of shrimp soup
1 green bell pepper, chopped	2 pounds shrimp
1 can reduced fat cream of mushroom soup	1 can Rotel tomatoes, undrained
1 can reduced fat cream of celery soup	

Sauté onion and bell pepper in skillet sprayed with nonstick cooking spray. Add soups, shrimp, and Rotel. Simmer until well blended. Place in casserole dish and bake at 350° for 30 minutes.

Yield: 8 servings
❦ *Calories: 185*
❦ *Fat: 5 grams*

Reduced Fat Seafood Spaghetti

Great served over whole wheat spaghetti or brown rice!

1 pound cooked shrimp	1 (8-ounce) can tomato sauce
2 cups frozen vegetable blend (onion, bell pepper, celery)	1 cup water/stock
1 tablespoon margarine	1 teaspoon salt
½ cup mushrooms	¼ teaspoon black pepper
2 tablespoons minced garlic	1 teaspoon basil
½ cup reduced fat mushroom soup	1 pound cooked crawfish tails
1 can Rotel tomatoes, chopped	red pepper, if desired
1 (6-ounce) can tomato paste	½ cup parsley
	green onion tops

Boil shrimp; reserve broth. Sauté vegetables in margarine. Add mushrooms and garlic. Sauté until tender. Add remaining ingredients, except parsley and green onion tops. Simmer 30 minutes. Cook pasta in shrimp broth for added flavor. Add parsley and green onions to sauce prior to serving.

Yield: 12 servings
❦ *Calories: 115 (without pasta)*
❦ *Fat: 3 grams*

Reduced Fat Seafood Enchiladas

This is a quick and easy recipe to impress friends and family when they come to your home for dinner. It reminds me a lot of the Reduced Fat Crawfish Etouffee that I made years ago on the show.

2   tablespoons reduced fat margarine

1   bunch green onions, sliced

1   pound peeled shrimp or 12 ounces crawfish tails

4   ounces green chilies

1   (4-ounce) jar diced pimentos

1   can reduced fat cream of mushroom soup

1   can cream of shrimp soup

1   (8-ounces) package light cream cheese, softened

salt and pepper to taste

10   (8-inch) wheat or flour tortillas

reduced fat or fat free shredded cheese of your choice (not included in nutritional information)

(Continued on next page.)

Sauté onions with margarine, add shrimp or crawfish; continue to sauté until tender. Add chilies, ½ jar of pimentos, reserving other half for garnish. Stir in soups, cream cheese, and salt and pepper. Stir over medium heat until cheese is melted and mixture is smooth. Spoon 2-3 tablespoons mixture in the center of each tortilla. Roll tortilla placing seam side down. Garnish with small amount of remaining mixture, shredded cheese, and pimentos. May warm each tortilla in microwave for about 30 seconds or bake at 325° for 20-30 minutes.

Yield: 10 servings
❦ *Calories: 175 (shrimp) 190 (crawfish)*
❦ *Fat: 8 grams (shrimp) 8 grams (crawfish)*

Low Fat Jambalaya

2   tablespoons oleo or butter
1   box Rice-A-Roni
2⅓ cups hot water
¼   teaspoon black pepper
¼   teaspoon Tabasco Pepper Sauce
1   tablespoon minced onion
2   teaspoons Kitchen Bouquet
½   cup diced celery
½   cup diced green bell pepper
1   pound fresh shelled shrimp
1   pound crawfish

Melt margarine in nonstick skillet. Add Rice-A-Roni (rice only) and sauté to a light brown. Stir in hot water. Add chicken flavor packet from Rice-A-Roni, plus black pepper, Tabasco, onion, Kitchen Bouquet, celery, and bell pepper. Add fresh shelled shrimp and crawfish. Cover and simmer for 15 minutes.

Yield: 8 servings
❧ *Calories: 195*
❧ *Fat: 4 grams*

Couscous with Shrimp

*This recipe was demonstrated on my
"Just Ask Stacey" cooking segment by Ruston,
Louisiana native Elizabeth Phillips, while she was
a Nutrition and Dietetics student at
Louisiana State University.*

1½ cups water
1 cup uncooked couscous
⅓ cup diced red bell pepper
2 tablespoons chopped fresh mint
½ pound medium shrimp, cooked and peeled
1 (10-ounce) package frozen green peas, thawed
½ cup thinly sliced green onions
¼ cup low-salt chicken broth
3 tablespoons white wine vinegar
1½ tablespoons extra-virgin olive oil
½ teaspoon sugar
½ teaspoon salt
½ teaspoon coarsely ground black pepper

Bring water to a boil in a medium saucepan. Stir in couscous. Remove from heat. Cover and let stand 5 minutes. Fluff with fork. Combine couscous, green onions, bell pepper, mint, shrimp, and green peas in a medium bowl; set aside. Combine broth, vinegar, olive oil, sugar, salt, and black pepper. Stir well with whisk. Pour dressing over couscous mixture. Toss gently to coat.

Yield: 6 servings
❦ *Calories: 250*
❦ *Fat: 5 grams*

Reduced Fat Crawfish Pie

For a great crawfish fettuccine, delete bread crumbs and add liquid (i.e. chicken broth) to desired consistency. Serve filling over hot fettuccine pasta.

1 cup chopped onion	1 teaspoon Tabasco Pepper Sauce
½ cup chopped green bell pepper	Tony Chachere's Original Seasoning
½ cup chopped celery	salt and pepper to taste
½ cup liquid Butter Buds	⅛ cup chopped parsley
2 teaspoons chopped/ minced garlic	1 pound crawfish tails
	2 teaspoons cornstarch
1 can reduced fat cream of mushroom soup	1 small can evaporated skim milk
1 can reduced fat cream of celery soup	2 (9-inch) pie shells
1 teaspoon Worcestershire sauce	¾ cup seasoned bread crumbs

Preheat oven to 350°. In large skillet, sauté vegetables in liquid Butter Buds. Add garlic, soups, seasonings, parsley, and crawfish tails. In separate bowl, blend cornstarch and milk; then add to mixture. Cook filling over medium heat about 10 minutes, stirring constantly, until well blended. Remove from heat and add bread crumbs. Mix well. Fill two pie shells evenly. Bake 35-45 minutes or until golden brown.

Yield: 16 servings
❧ *Calories: 175*
❧ *Fat: 6 grams*

Low Fat Crawfish Enchiladas

½ cup chopped green bell pepper
2 tablespoons chopped jalapeno pepper
1 onion, chopped
1 teaspoon onion powder
1 pound crawfish
1 cup evaporated skim milk
1 can cream of shrimp soup

½ cup shredded reduced fat sharp cheese
½ cup shredded fat free mozzarella cheese
1 package enchilada seasoning
1 small can tomato sauce
½ cup water
8 corn tortillas

Garnish:

½ cup chopped green onion   shredded cheese

Sauté peppers and onion; add onion powder and crawfish. Continue to sauté until tender. Add milk, soup, and cheese. In separate bowl, combine enchilada seasoning, tomato sauce, and water. Heat in microwave. Dip each corn tortilla in hot enchilada sauce. Fill tortillas with crawfish mixture. Place rolled enchiladas in casserole dish. Add enchilada sauce to remaining cream sauce from crawfish mixture. Pour combined mixture over enchiladas. Garnish with green onions and a small amount of cheese.

Yield: 8 servings
❦ *Calories: 235 (without garnish)*
❦ *Fat: 5 grams*

Low Fat
Crawfish Casserole

½ cup liquid Butter Buds	2 small cans Rotel tomatoes
½ cup chopped green bell pepper	1½ cans water
½ cup chopped onion	2 cups raw rice
1 small can reduced fat cream of chicken soup	1 pound crawfish tails, cooked, peeled & deveined
1 small can French onion soup	

Place Butter Buds in bottom of large casserole dish. Add all ingredients and mix well. Bake uncovered at 375° for 15 minutes; remove and stir well. Cover and bake an additional 30 minutes or until liquid is absorbed.

Yield: 12 servings of about 1 cup each
❦ *Calories: 155*
❦ *Fat: 1 gram*

Reduced Fat Stuffed Catfish

1 cup chopped onion
2 cans shrimp, rinsed and drained
1 (4½-ounce) jar sliced mushrooms, drained
2 tablespoons reduced fat margarine
2 cans crab meat or ½ pound crab meat

8 catfish fillets
   salt, pepper, and paprika to taste
2 cans reduced fat cream of mushroom soup
⅓ cup chicken broth
2 tablespoons water

Garnish:

shredded reduced fat or fat free cheddar cheese

parsley

In a skillet, sauté onion, shrimp, and mushrooms in margarine until onion is tender. Add crab meat; heat through. Sprinkle fillets with salt, pepper, and paprika. Spoon shrimp mixture on fillets; roll up and fasten with a toothpick. Place in a prepared 13 × 9-inch baking dish. In a separate bowl combine soup, broth, and water, blending until smooth. Pour soup mixture over fillets. Sprinkle each fillet with a small amount of cheese. Cover and bake at 400° for 30 minutes. Remove from oven, sprinkle with parsley and return, uncovered, to oven for 5 minutes,

Yield: 8 servings
❦ *Calories: 225 (without garnish)*
❦ *Fat: 10 grams*

Low Fat Picante Rice with Fish

3 (4-ounce) whole catfish filets
Nature's Seasons Pepper, Onion, Garlic, Parsley, and Celery Blend
paprika, thyme
2 stalks celery, diced
½ cup red sweet peppers, diced

1 cup sliced mushrooms
1 tablespoon cold water
1 tablespoon cornstarch
2 cups brown rice, cooked
½ cup picante sauce

Place catfish in large saucepan and add just enough water to cover. Add the seasonings and vegetables. Simmer for about 10 minutes or until fish is cooked. In small bowl, blend together cornstarch and cold water. Add cornstarch mixture to saucepan, and stir until slightly thick. Mix cooked rice with catfish and sauce, gently blending to prevent fish from breaking apart. Serve hot.

Yield: 6 servings (½ whole fish and ½ cup rice mixture)
❦ *Calories: 240*
❦ *Fat: 2 grams*

Reduced Fat Catfish Parmesan

This recipe works with chicken, too!

6-8 skinned catfish
(fresh or frozen)
1 cup dry bread
crumbs
¾ cup grated
Parmesan cheese
¼ cup chopped parsley
1 teaspoon paprika

½ teaspoon oregano
¼ teaspoon leaf basil
2 teaspoons salt
½ teaspoon pepper
½ cup yellow mustard
lemon wedges
parsley springs

Thaw fish if frozen. Clean, wash, and dry fish. Combine bread crumbs, Parmesan cheese, parsley, paprika, oregano, basil, salt, and pepper. Dip catfish in mustard and roll in crumb mixture. Arrange fish in a well greased 13 × 9 × 2-inch baking dish. Bake at 375° about 25 minutes or until fish flakes easily when tested with a fork. Garnish with a lemon wedge and parsley.

Yield: 6-8 servings
❦ *Calories: 95*
❦ *Fat: 3 grams*

Catfish Courtbouillion

1 pound catfish fillets
lemon pepper to taste
cayenne pepper to taste
garlic powder to taste
¼ cup reduced fat
   margarine
1 onion, chopped

1 green pepper,
   chopped
2 stalks celery, chopped
1 can diced Rotel
   tomatoes
1 can tomato sauce
1 lemon, sliced

Season fish to taste. Set aside. In a large saucepan, melt margarine and add onions, pepper, and celery. Sauté for 10 minutes, adding water as necessary to prevent seasoning from burning. Once onions are transparent, add tomatoes and tomato sauce. Reduce heat and simmer for 30-45 minutes, adding water as necessary. After sauce has cooked, add catfish fillets and simmer for 20 minutes. (Do not stir, or the fish will fall apart.) Serve with slice of lemon over hot rice.

Yield: 4 servings
❦ *Calories: 210*
❦ *Fat: 9 grams*

Easy Low Fat Etouffee

*Etouffee is a Louisiana specialty. This recipe is
so easy, but your friends will think you've been
to a New Orleans culinary school!*

1 large onion, chopped	1 can reduced fat
1 large green bell	cream of celery soup
pepper, chopped	2 cans Rotel tomatoes
1 pound crawfish	¼ teaspoon red pepper
1 pound shrimp	½ teaspoon minced
2 tablespoons reduced	garlic
fat margarine	½ teaspoon onion
1 can cream of shrimp	powder
soup	2 tablespoons minced
1 can reduced fat cream	parsley
of mushroom soup	salt and pepper to taste

Spray skillet with nonstick cooking spray. Add
onions and peppers and sauté. Allow vegetables to
cook until tender, adding water as needed. Add
crawfish and shrimp. Cover and allow to simmer
10 minutes. Add margarine, soups, tomatoes, and
seasonings. Pour into slow cooker and simmer for
1-2 hours.

Yield: 12 servings
❦ Calories: 130
❦ Fat: 4 grams

Low Fat Venison Chili

2 pounds venison
1 large onion, chopped
2 cloves garlic, minced
2 cans Rotel tomatoes, chopped
1 can tomato sauce
2 teaspoons granulated sugar
1 can water

4 tablespoons chili powder
2 tablespoons paprika
1 teaspoon red pepper
1 tablespoon ground cumin
1 teaspoon oregano
salt and pepper to taste

Spray nonstick skillet with cooking spray. Brown meat and drain. Add onion and garlic and sauté for about five minutes. Add remaining ingredients and simmer about two hours or until meat is tender.

Yield: 8 servings
❦ *Calories: 265*
❦ *Fat: 4 grams*

Reduced Fat Mexican Stew

*This stew is delicious served with
shredded Mexican cheese blend.*

1 pound lean venison,
  cut into small cubes
1½ cups diced onions
4 tablespoons minced
  garlic
1 (15-ounce) can
  pinto beans with
  jalapeno peppers
1 (15-ounce) can
  ranch style beans
1 (15-ounce) can
  golden hominy
  with red and
  green peppers

1 (11-ounce) can
  Mexican-style corn
1 (14-ounce) can
  stewed tomatoes,
  Mexican recipe
1 (10-ounce) can
  Rotel tomatoes,
  Mexican style
2 teaspoons cumin
3 cups beef broth

Combine all ingredients. Cook in a slow cooker all day. If time does not allow, cover meat with water and add ½ cup onions and 2 tablespoons minced garlic. Boil until tender and reserve 3 cups broth. In a large saucepan, sauté remaining onions and garlic; add boiled meat. Add remaining ingredients. Bring to a boil. Reduce heat and simmer, uncovered, for 1 hour.

Yield: 10 servings
❦ *Calories: 235*
❦ *Fat: 5 grams*

"Moderation & the richness of life go together. Moderation is self-discipline born from a desire to make lasting changes in our lives. We can all enjoy the richness of life without compromising our health."

DESSERTS

"Have Your King Cake and Eat It Too!"

Stacey's Low Fat Coconut Cake

1 box reduced fat
   white cake mix
1 (9-ounce) container
   fat free Cool Whip
1 cup granulated
   sugar

½ cup skim milk
1 teaspoon coconut
   extract
⅓ cup flaked coconut

Prepare cake batter according to box directions, substituting applesauce and Egg Beaters for oil and eggs. Bake cake in 9 × 13-inch pan and let cool. Mix sugar and milk; bring to a boil. Let boil 1 minute. Remove from heat and add coconut flavoring. With fork, poke holes in top of cooled cake. Pour filling over cake. Cool. Spread Cool Whip over top and sprinkle with flaked coconut. Keep refrigerated.

Yield: 16 servings
❦ *Calories: 240*
❦ *Fat: 2 grams*

Low Fat Devil's Food Surprise

1 box reduced fat
   devil's food cake mix
1⅓ cups water
4 large egg whites
½ teaspoon butter
   extract
4 ounces fat free
   cream cheese

¼ cup fat free
   margarine
1 cup powdered sugar
¼ teaspoon vanilla
   extract
¼ teaspoon butter
   extract

Icing:

⅔ cup granulated sugar
⅓ cup fat free sour
   cream

1½ cups Cool Whip

Prepare cake mix and bake in two round pans according to directions, using water, egg whites, and butter flavoring as substitutions. Place on cooling rack and set aside until cooled. To prepare filling, beat cream cheese and margarine together. Add powdered sugar and extracts and beat until smooth. Place one cooled cake layer on serving platter. Using the handle of a wooden spoon, poke holes in cake and fill with filling. Place second layer on top of first layer; poke holes in second layer and fill with filling. Combine icing ingredients and spread over entire cake. Refrigerate before serving. After icing has set, decorate cake with fresh fruit.

Yield: 16 servings
❦ *Calories: 215*
❦ *Fat: 2.5 grams*

Low Fat Strawberry Cake with Strawberry Dream Icing

1 box white cake mix
1 small box sugar free strawberry gelatin
1 cup fresh strawberries, mashed
¾ cup applesauce
¼ cup reduced fat margarine, melted
½ cup skim milk
1 cup fat free Egg Beaters

Preheat oven to 350°. Prepare 13 × 9-inch cake pan with nonstick cooking spray. Combine all ingredients in a large mixing bowl. Beat with electric mixer about 4 minutes or until well blended. Bake for 35-40 minutes or until cake is light brown. Let cool completely before frosting.

Yield: 16 servings
❦ *Calories: 165*
❦ *Fat: 4 grams*

Fat Free Strawberry Dream Icing

1½ cups skim milk
1 envelope Dream Whip
1 small box sugar free instant vanilla pudding mix
8 ounces fat free cream cheese, softened
1 teaspoon strawberry extract
1 cup fresh strawberries, mashed

Pour milk into mixing bowl. Add Dream Whip and pudding mix; beat with electric mixer on high for about 4 minutes or until mixture forms soft peaks. In a separate bowl blend the cream cheese until softened. Add to topping mixture. Fold in extract and strawberries. Spread the frosting on cooled cake.

Yield: 16 servings
❦ *Calories: 55*
❦ *Fat: 0 grams*

Low Fat Coffee Cake

¼ cup pecans	¾ cup granulated sugar
4 tablespoons reduced fat margarine, melted	4 ounces reduced fat cream cheese
2-3 teaspoons orange extract	2 cans low fat biscuits

Glaze:

1 cup sifted powdered sugar	2 tablespoons fresh orange juice

Preheat oven to 350°. Lightly spray Bundt pan with nonstick cooking spray. Place pecans in bottom of pan. Combine melted margarine with orange extract in a small bowl. Place sugar in separate small bowl. Separate biscuits and spread about 1 teaspoon cream cheese on half of each biscuit. Fold each biscuit over cheese, pressing edges to seal. Dip biscuits in melted margarine, then in granulated sugar. Place folded biscuits curved side down in Bundt pan, spacing evenly. Drizzle any remaining sugar or margarine on top before baking. Bake at 350° for 30 minutes or until done. Immediately invert cake onto serving plate. Combine powdered sugar and orange juice; stir well and drizzle over coffee cake. Serve immediately.

Yield: 20 servings
❦ *Calories: 100*
❦ *Fat: 3 grams*

Low Fat Blueberry Pound Cake

1 box reduced fat yellow cake mix	1 teaspoon butter extract
1 cup water	8 ounces fat free cream cheese
¾ cup fat free Egg Beaters	¼ cup granulated sugar
½ cup liquid Butter Buds	2 cups fresh blueberries

Beat cake mix, water, Egg Beaters, Butter Buds, and butter extract. In separate bowl, combine cream cheese and sugar; blend well. Add to cake batter. Fold in 2 cups blueberries. Pour in 12-cup Bundt pan prepared with nonstick cooking spray. Bake at 350° for 1 hour or until golden brown.

Yield: 12 servings
❦ *Calories: 225*
❦ *Fat: 2 grams*

Low Fat Apricot Nectar Cake

This cake is a compact cake, but what it lacks in size it certainly makes up in taste! Hope you enjoy it as much as I do.

1 box lemon cake mix with pudding	1 teaspoon vanilla extract
6 ounces apricot juice	1 cup granulated sugar
½ cup liquid Butter Buds	4 egg whites

Glaze:

1 cup powdered sugar   juice of 1½ fresh lemons

Preheat oven to 350°. Combine dry cake mix, apricot juice, Butter Buds, vanilla, and sugar in large mixing bowl. Beat with electric mixer at medium speed for 2 minutes or until well blended. Beat egg whites separately and fold into batter. Pour into Bundt pan sprayed with nonstick cooking spray. Bake at 350° for about 35-40 minutes. Let cake cool several minutes in pan before turning onto serving plate. Combine powdered sugar and lemon juice to form glaze. After cake has cooled completely, drizzle with glaze and serve.

Yield: 24 servings
❦ *Calories: 150*
❦ *Fat: 2 grams*

Low Fat Apple Spice Cake

2¾ cups unsifted
    all-purpose flour
1¼ cups granulated
    sugar
2½ teaspoons baking
    soda
1¼ teaspoons baking
    powder
2 teaspoons cinnamon
1 teaspoon nutmeg

1 teaspoon salt
¼ teaspoon cloves
1¾ cups applesauce
1¼ cup plain nonfat
    yogurt
½ cup Egg Beaters
⅓ cup reduced fat
    margarine
1 cup raisins

In a large bowl, thoroughly combine flour, sugar, baking soda, baking powder, cinnamon, nutmeg, salt, and cloves. Add applesauce, yogurt, Egg Beaters, and reduced fat margarine; blend well using spoon. Stir in raisins. Pour into greased and floured 12-cup Bundt or 13 × 9-inch pan. Bake at 325° for 50-60 minutes or until toothpick inserted in center comes out clean. Cool 15 minutes. Loosen cake from sides of pan with knife. Invert onto plate. Cover loosely with foil or wax paper. Cool completely.

Yield: 16 servings
❧ *Calories: less than 200*
❧ *Fat: less than 1 gram*

Light Lemon Cake

1   lemon supreme
    cake mix
1   small box fat free
    lemon instant
    pudding

¾   cup fat free Egg
    Beaters
⅓   cup applesauce
8   ounces Sprite
1   teaspoon vanilla
    extract

Combine first 4 ingredients; beat with electric mixer on low speed until well blended. In small saucepan over medium heat, bring Sprite to a boil; add vanilla extract. With mixer on low speed, gradually add hot Sprite into batter. Continue beating batter on medium speed for 2 minutes. Pour batter into Bundt pan sprayed with nonstick cooking spray. Bake at 350° for about 30 minutes.

Yield: 16 servings
❦ *Calories: 160*
❦ *Fat: 3 grams*

Fat Free Pear Cake

This cake will stay fresh for several days
if stored in a sealed container.

3 cups peeled and chopped pears	½ cup liquid Butter Buds
2 tablespoons lemon juice	1 teaspoon soda
2 cups granulated sugar	3 cups flour
4 egg whites	2 teaspoons cinnamon
½ cup applesauce	2 teaspoons nutmeg
2 teaspoons vanilla extract	2 teaspoons baking powder
	1 (8-ounce) box diced dates

Place pears in medium bowl; add lemon juice and sugar. Let stand 20 minutes or more. Beat egg whites until peaks form; add applesauce, vanilla, and liquid Butter Buds. Mix well. In separate bowl, sift all dry ingredients together. Add dry ingredients to egg white mixture; fold in pears and dates. Pour batter into Bundt pan prepared with nonstick cooking spray. Bake at 350° for 1½ hours. Let cool before removing from pan.

Yield: 24 servings
❦ *Calories: 168*
❦ *Fat: 0 grams*

Low Fat Hummingbird Cake

*For an easy garnish, melt two tablespoons
prepared cream cheese icing and
drizzle over cooled cake.*

¾ cup Egg Beaters
1 cup granulated sugar
3 cups plain flour
1 cup applesauce
½ cup plain yogurt
1 teaspoon vanilla
    extract
1 teaspoon butter
    extract

1 (8-ounce) can
    crushed pineapple,
    drained
2 bananas, mashed
1 teaspoon baking
    soda
1 teaspoon cinnamon
½ cup chopped nuts

Beat Egg Beaters with sugar; add remaining
ingredients and mix well. Bake in greased and
floured tube pan at 350° for 45-50 minutes.

Yield: 16 servings
❦ *Calories: 185*
❦ *Fat: 3 grams*

Low Fat Honey Bun Cake

1 box reduced fat yellow cake mix	¼ cup reduced fat margarine
1 cup fat free Egg Beaters	8 ounces fat free sour cream
1 cup water	1 teaspoon butter extract

Filling:

½ cup brown sugar	1 tablespoon granulated sugar
1 teaspoon cinnamon	

Icing:

1 cup powdered sugar	3 tablespoons margarine, melted

Prepare a 9 × 13-inch pan with nonstick cooking spray. Mix cake ingredients well and pour ½ batter into pan. Combine brown sugar, cinnamon, and granulated sugar and mix well. Sprinkle ½ mixture over batter. Pour remaining batter over sugar mixture. Sprinkle remaining sugar mixture over batter, using a fork to swirl into batter. Bake at 350° for about 25 minutes or until done. Do not overbake. While cake is still hot, combine powdered sugar and melted margarine. Poke small holes in cake with fork and drizzle icing over cake.

Yield: 16 servings
❦ *Calories: 225*
❦ *Fat: 3 grams*

Low Fat "No Pound" Cake

For an easy glaze, combine 1 cup powdered sugar, ½ teaspoon vanilla extract, and 1 tablespoon milk. Try serving cake with fresh or frozen strawberries and fat free Cool Whip for a wonderful strawberry shortcake.

1	box reduced fat white cake mix	1	cup fat free Egg Beaters
½	cup granulated sugar	1	teaspoon butter extract
¾	cup fat free sour cream	1	teaspoon vanilla extract
¼	cup light sour cream		
¼	cup reduced fat margarine		

Combine cake mix, sugar, sour cream, and margarine; beat until creamy. Slowly add Egg Beaters, beating after each addition. Add extracts. Beat for 5 minutes. Spray Bundt pan with nonstick cooking spray. Pour batter into pan and bake at 350° for 30-35 minutes or until done.

Yield: 16 servings
❦ Calories: 180
❦ Fat: 3 grams

Low Fat Peach Cake

1	cup sliced peaches (fresh or frozen)	½	cup light applesauce
2	tablespoons granulated sugar	3	tablespoons reduced fat margarine
1	box yellow cake mix	¾	cup fat free Egg Beaters
1	small box peach gelatin	½	cup skim milk

Glaze:

1½ cups powdered sugar   reserved peach juice
2 tablespoons   milk to thin if necessary
   margarine,melted

Add 2 tablespoons sugar to peaches; set aside. Mix cake mix, dry gelatin, applesauce, margarine, Egg Beaters, and milk. Beat 4 minutes. Drain peaches, reserving juice. Stir in peaches and pour mixture into Bundt pan. Bake at 350° for 35 minutes. Combine glaze ingredients and pour onto cooled cake.

Yield: 24 servings
❦ *Calories: 115 (without glaze)*
❦ *Fat: 2 grams (without glaze)*

Low Fat Strawberry Supreme Cake

1   box reduced fat white cake mix
1   (3-ounce) box sugar free strawberry gelatin
½   cup liquid Butter Buds
¾   cup skim milk
2   tablespoons flour

2   cups frozen strawberries, thawed
4   egg whites
1   container reduced fat vanilla frosting
½   cup fresh strawberries (garnish)

Preheat oven to 350°. Combine cake mix and all ingredients except egg whites. Beat cake mixture until smooth. In separate bowl, beat egg whites until stiff. Fold egg whites into cake mixture. Spray two round cake pans with nonstick cooking spray. Pour mixture into pans and bake for about 25 minutes. Spread frosting over cooled cake and garnish with strawberries.

Yield: 16 servings
❦ *Calories: 250*
❦ *Fat: 3 grams*

Low Fat
Sweet Potato Cake

1 cup fat free Egg Beaters
4 cups fresh sweet potatoes, mashed; or 2 (16-ounce) cans pumpkin
1 cup granulated sugar
2 (12-ounce) cans evaporated skim milk
1 teaspoon cinnamon
2 teaspoons vanilla extract
1 teaspoon butter extract
dash salt
1 box reduced fat yellow cake mix
½ cup reduced fat margarine, melted

Spray an 11 × 15-inch pan or 2 medium baking pans with nonstick cooking spray. Beat Egg Beaters, sweet potatoes, sugar, milk, cinnamon, extracts, and salt until well blended. Pour mixture into prepared pan. Sprinkle top with dry cake mix and drizzle with melted margarine. Bake at 350° for 1 hour and 25 minutes.

Yield: 24 servings
❦ *Calories: 150*
❦ *Fat: 2½ grams*

No Sugar Added Pineapple Surprise Cake

You may also use a frozen reduced fat pound cake with this recipe. Thaw before assembly. Nutritional information is for angel food cake.

1 large box sugar free vanilla instant pudding mix
1 (16-ounce) prepared angel food cake
½ cup pineapple juice
1 teaspoon almond extract
1 (20-ounce) can crushed pineapple, drained
12 ounces fat free Cool Whip
¼ cup toasted slivered almonds

Prepare pudding using skim milk according to box directions. Set aside. Cut cake horizontally into 3 layers. Drizzle with mixture of pineapple juice and almond flavoring. Combine pineapple and prepared pudding in bowl; mix well. Fold in whipped topping. Spread between layers and over top and sides of cake. Sprinkle with almonds.

Yield: 12 servings
❦ *Calories: 200*
❦ *Fat: 2 grams*

Punch Bowl Cake

Serves a crowd!

1 prepared angel food cake
2 small boxes sugar free vanilla pudding mix
2 (20-ounce) cans light cherry pie filling
1 (20-ounce) can pineapple, in its own juice, drained
1 (16-ounce) container fat free Cool Whip
1/3 cup chopped pecans

Prepare pudding according to box directions; set aside. Crumble 1/3 cake into bottom of clear bowl. Add 1/3 pudding, pie filling, pineapple, whipped topping, and pecans. Repeat layers 2 more times, ending with whipped topping and pecans. Chill before serving.

Yield: 24 servings
❦ *Calories: 145*
❦ *Fat: 2 grams*

Reduced Fat and Calorie Turtle Cake

This cake is just as delicious as the high calorie/high fat version, which has 400 calories and 14 fat grams per serving!

1   box reduced fat devil's food cake mix
1   can fat free sweetened condensed milk
1   jar fat free caramel ice cream topping
8   ounces light Cool Whip
2   tablespoons Heath Bar bits

Bake cake according to low cholesterol instructions, using only egg whites. When done, remove from oven and poke holes in cake with the end of a wooden spoon or a large meat fork. Mix condensed milk and caramel topping together and pour ½ of the mixture over hot cake, reserving the other half in the refrigerator to use later. Refrigerate cake until cold. Top with Cool Whip and sprinkle with Heath bits.

Yield: 16 servings
❦ *Calories: 244*
❦ *Fat: 4 grams*

Reduced Fat Chocolate Chip Pound Cake

1 box yellow cake mix
1 small box sugar free instant chocolate pudding mix
½ cup applesauce
1 cup fat free Egg Beaters
1 cup water
1 cup light sour cream
1 cup reduced fat chocolate chips

Combine dry ingredients in mixing bowl. Add remaining ingredients, except chocolate chips, and mix with electric mixer on medium speed. Fold in chocolate chips. Pour into prepared Bundt pan. Bake at 350° for 45 minutes.

Yield: 16 servings
❦ *Calories: 155*
❦ *Fat: 5 grams*

Reduced Fat Chocolate Cola Cake

1 box devil's food cake mix (without pudding)
1 large box fat free instant chocolate pudding mix
1 cup fat free Egg Beaters
½ cup liquid Butter Buds
1 teaspoon butter extract
1 (8-ounce) bottle Coke

Chocolate Cola Frosting:

¼ cup reduced fat margarine
3 tablespoons Coke
1½ tablespoons cocoa
2 cups powdered sugar
1 teaspoon vanilla extract

Combine cake mix, pudding mix, Egg Beaters, Butter Buds, and butter extract and beat on low speed until well blended; set aside. Bring Coke to a boil in a small saucepan over medium heat. With mixer on low speed, gradually add hot Coke into batter. Beat on medium speed for 2 minutes. Pour batter into Bundt pan sprayed with nonstick cooking spray. Bake at 350° for about 30 minutes. For frosting, combine margarine, 3 tablespoons Coke, and cocoa in small saucepan. Cook over medium heat, stirring constantly, until margarine melts. Do not boil. Remove from heat and add powdered sugar and vanilla, stirring until smooth. Spread frosting over cooled cake.

Yield: 12 servings
❦ *Calories: 310*
❦ *Fat: 5.5 grams*

Reduced Fat Mandarin Orange Cake

1 box yellow cake mix
1 cup fat free Egg Beaters
½ cup liquid Butter Buds

1 (11-ounce) can mandarin oranges with juice

Icing:

8 ounces light Cool Whip
1 large can crushed pineapple in its own juice

1 (1½-ounce) box sugar free vanilla instant pudding mix

Combine cake ingredients. Mix 2-3 minutes or until well blended. Pour into 2 round 9-inch cake pans. Bake at 350° for 18-20 minutes. Prepare icing by combining dry pudding and pineapple, including juice. Fold in Cool Whip and spread onto cooled cake. Refrigerate after icing.

Yield: 16 servings
❦ *Calories: 220*
❦ *Fat: 5 grams*

Reduced Fat Poppy Seed Cake

This cake is delicious warmed in the microwave and served as a coffee cake at breakfast.

1 box yellow butter cake mix	5 tablespoons reduced fat margarine, melted
½ cup granulated sugar	1 cup Egg Beaters
½ cup liquid Butter Buds	1 cup light sour cream
1 teaspoon butter extract	¼ cup poppy seeds

Combine cake mix, sugar, liquid Butter Buds, butter extract, and melted margarine. Add Egg Beaters. Fold in sour cream; add poppy seeds. Pour into prepared Bundt pan or two loaf pans. Bake at 350° for about 45 minutes.

Yield: 20 servings
❦ *Calories: 200*
❦ *Fat: 5 grams*

Reduced Fat Rum Cake

⅓ cup pecans, crushed
1 box yellow cake mix
1 small box fat free sugar free instant vanilla pudding mix
1 teaspoon rum extract
1 teaspoon vanilla extract
1 cup fat free Egg Beaters
1 cup water
⅓ cup applesauce
1 tablespoon melted margarine

Glaze:

⅓ cup margarine
½ cup granulated sugar
¼ cup water
2 teaspoons rum

Prepare Bundt pan with nonstick cooking spray. Sprinkle pecans in bottom of pan. Mix remaining ingredients and pour batter over pecans. Bake at 350° for 30 minutes or until done. Remove from oven and pierce holes in cake with toothpick or skewer. To prepare glaze, boil first 3 ingredients 3-5 minutes, stirring constantly. Add flavoring. Pour ½ hot glaze over top of cake. Do not remove from pan until cake is completely cooled. Drizzle and smooth remaining glaze evenly over top of cake. Allow cake to absorb glaze before serving.

Yield: 16 servings
❦ *Calories: 210*
❦ *Fat: 4 grams*

Reduced Fat "So Easy" Cake

This cake is great topped with fat free Cool Whip. For variety, use a butterscotch or vanilla pudding, a caramel cake mix, and butterscotch chips!

1   small box sugar free chocolate pudding mix (not instant)
1   box chocolate cake mix

½   cup semisweet chocolate pieces
½   cup chopped nuts

Prepare pudding according to box directions and blend dry cake mix into hot pudding (mixture will be thick). Pour into prepared 9 × 13-inch pan and sprinkle with chocolate pieces and nuts. Bake at 350° for 30 to 35 minutes. Let cool before serving.

Yield: 24 servings
❦ *Calories: 145*
❦ *Fat: 5 grams*

Victoria & Elizabeth-Kate's Reduced Fat Coke Float Cake

1   box white cake mix
8   ounces Coke
4   tablespoons cocoa powder

¼   cup reduced fat margarine, melted
2   eggs
1   teaspoon vanilla extract

Glaze:

¼   cup Coke

½   cup reduced fat chocolate icing

Combine cake ingredients in a large mixing bowl; beat mixture at low speed with an electric mixer until moistened. Use spatula to rake sides of bowl; beat at medium speed for about 2 minutes. Pour into Bundt pan prepared with nonstick cooking spray. Bake about 35 minutes or until center is firm. Cool in pan on a wire rack; remove from pan. Pierce top of cake with a long wooden or metal skewer. To prepare glaze, bring Coke to a boil, stir in icing and continue stirring until melted. Drizzle cake with glaze or icing of your choice. Serve cooled cake with fat free vanilla ice cream.

Yield: 16 servings
❧ *Calories: 180 (does not include glaze or icing)*
❧ *Fat: 6 grams*

Fat Free Banana Split Cake

1 reduced fat yellow cake mix
2 tablespoons Smuckers Baking Replacement or applesauce
1⅓ cups water
¾ cup Egg Beaters
1 teaspoon butter extract

1 package instant vanilla pudding mix
3 cups skim milk
1 (15½-ounce) can crushed pineapple
3 bananas, sliced
12 ounces fat free Cool Whip
14 cherries

Prepare cake batter using oil replacement, 1⅓ cups water, and Egg Beaters. Add 1 teaspoon butter extract to batter. Bake cake according to directions in a large casserole dish. Let cool. Prepare pudding using skim milk and set aside. Warm pineapple and pour over cake. Place banana slices over pineapple layer. Spread pudding, then Cool Whip. Garnish with cherries. Chill.

Yield: 24 servings
❦ *Calories: 160*
❦ *Fat: less than one gram*

Reduced Fat Ruston Peach Cake

We are blessed to live in the South, especially in the summer with the abundance of fresh fruits. The Peach Festival in Ruston, Louisiana has always marked the true beginning of summer for my family. To us there is nothing better on a hot summer day than a good, sweet peach (other than a Saline watermelon, of course!)

7	small to medium Ruston peaches	1	box reduced fat yellow cake mix
1	tablespoon lemon juice	1	teaspoon butter extract
½	cup granulated sugar		

Frosting:

1	cup skim milk	1	large can crushed pineapple, drained
1	large box sugar free instant vanilla pudding	½	cup chopped pecans
8	ounces light Cool Whip		

Peel and dice peaches into 1 tablespoon lemon juice. Add ½ cup sugar and toss. Set aside. Prepare cake mix according to package directions for low fat/low cholesterol method. Add butter extract. Add juice from diced peaches, about ¾ cup, omitting water called for in directions. When mixed well, fold in peaches. Divide batter into 4 cake pans sprayed with nonstick cooking spray. Bake at 350° for about 20 minutes. Cool completely before frosting. To make frosting, mix 1 cup cold skim milk with pudding mix and fold in Cool Whip, drained pineapple, and pecans. Frost layers and refrigerate before serving.

Yield: 16 servings
❦ *Calories: 280* ❦ *Fat: 5 grams*

Reduced Fat King Cake

*You can have your cake and eat it, too, with this
lower fat version of the popular Mardi Gras King
Cake. Make it festive with colored sugar, beads,
and the traditional plastic baby.*

2 cans reduced fat cinnamon rolls, with icing	¾ cup granulated sugar, divided into 3 parts of ¼ cup each
	food coloring

Filling:

4 ounces light cream cheese	1 tablespoon skim milk
½ cup powdered sugar	⅔ cup light cherry pie filling

Use food coloring to dye sugar green, purple, and yellow.
Separate one can of cinnamon rolls and roll each by hand
so that it looks like a hot dog. Place cinnamon rolls on a
cookie sheet sprayed with nonstick cooking spray.
Arrange rolls to form an oval shape, and pinch ends
together. Combine cream cheese, powdered sugar and
skim milk to make filling. Pat rolls down and spread
cream cheese filling on top; then add layer of cherry pie
filling. Separate second can of cinnamon rolls; roll, shape
and press to cover filling and form top layer of cake. Bake
at 375° for about 20 minutes. Top with icing from cans
and colored sugar.

Yield: 16 servings
❦ *Calories: 200*
❦ *Fat: 4½ fat grams*

Reduced Fat Popcorn Cake

This cake is great served at Halloween and garnished with a few orange candy-coated chocolate pieces.

3½ quarts (14 cups) popped popcorn
1 (6-ounce) package reduced fat chocolate chips
½ cup reduced fat margarine

½ cup reduced fat peanut butter
1 (10½-ounce) package miniature marshmallows

Line entire 12-cup fluted tube pan or 10-inch tube pan with aluminum foil. Spray foil with nonstick cooking spray. In 6-quart container or 2 large bowls, combine popcorn and chocolate chips; set aside. In medium saucepan, melt margarine. Stir in peanut butter and marshmallows. Cook over low heat until marshmallows are melted, stirring constantly. Pour marshmallow mixture over popcorn and chocolate chips; stir to coat. Press mixture firmly into foil-lined pan. Cool completely; remove from pan. Cut into slices to serve.

Yield: 16 servings
❦ *Calories: 210*
❦ *Fat: 6 grams*

Working Woman's Easy Rainbow Easter Cake

This recipe calls for 3 (9-inch) cake layers, which you can prepare using a reduced fat or regular cake mix. If using a regular cake mix, substitute reduced fat margarine or applesauce for oil, and fat free Egg Beaters for eggs. Add 1 teaspoon butter extract to batter. Monitor cooking time; cakes will cook faster due to reduction of fat in recipe. One box of cake mix makes 2 layers, so you will need two boxes to make 3 layers. You will have about ¼ batter remaining. This recipe is also great made with angel food cake!

3   baked 9-inch round (reduced fat) white cake layers, cooled
3   cups boiling water

3   small boxes sugar free gelatin (lemon, lime and strawberry)
1   (8-ounce) fat free Cool Whip, thawed

(Continued on next page.)

Remove cooled cakes from cake pans; place cake layers back in clean pans, top sides up. Pierce cakes with a large fork at ½-inch intervals. Stir 1 cup boiling water into each package of gelatin, stirring until completely dissolved. Carefully pour one flavor gelatin over each cake layer (one layer will be pink, yellow, and green after chilled). Refrigerate for a minimum of 3 hours. Turn one cake layer onto serving platter. (You may need to dip cake pans in warm water about 10 seconds to release from pan.) Spread with about 1 cup Cool Whip. Repeat with each layer, frosting top and sides with remaining Cool Whip. Refrigerate at least 1 hour before serving. Decorate as desired. Cake should be stored in refrigerator.

Yield: 24 servings
❦ *Calories: 165*
❦ *Fat: 3 grams*

St. Patrick's Day Pistachio Cake

This "green cake" is perfect to serve on St. Patrick's day. Make an extra one to give to someone special. They will count their blessings for a friend like you!

Cake Batter:

1   box yellow cake mix
1   small box pistachio pudding mix
¾   cup fat free Egg Beaters
⅓   cup applesauce
1   tablespoon reduced fat margarine, melted

1   cup water
1   cup fat free sour cream
1   teaspoon vanilla extract
1   teaspoon butter extract

Additions:

¼   cup small pecan pieces
¼   cup mini semisweet chocolate chips

¼   cup light chocolate syrup

(Continued on next page.)

Preheat oven to 350°. Prepare a 10-inch Bundt pan with nonstick cooking spray. In a mixing bowl, combine cake mix and remaining ingredients for cake batter. Blend with hand mixer until well blended, set aside. Sprinkle the prepared Bundt pan with pecan pieces and chocolate chips. Pour about ½ of batter into the pan, over the pecans and chocolate chips. Drizzle chocolate syrup on top of batter; spoon remaining batter into pan. Bake for 45 minutes or until done. Allow cake to cool before inverting onto serving platter. May garnish cake with small amount of chocolate syrup, drizzling syrup over cake and platter.

Yield: 16 servings
❦ *Calories: 235*
❦ *Fat: 5 grams*

Reduced Fat Strawberry Sweetheart Cake

1 box strawberry supreme cake mix	¾ cup fat free Egg Beaters
1 small box sugar free strawberry gelatin	½ cup liquid Butter Buds
1⅓ cups water	1 small package frozen strawberries, pureed

Frosting:

1 small box sugar free vanilla instant pudding mix	2 envelopes Dream Whip
1 cup skim milk	1 cup cold skim milk
	1 teaspoon vanilla extract

Preheat oven to 350°. Spray 2 round 8-inch or heart-shaped pans with nonstick cooking spray. Combine cake mix with strawberry gelatin. Add water, Egg Beaters, and Butter Buds. Blend all ingredients until moistened. Beat on medium speed for 2 minutes. Pour batter into pans and bake about 25 minutes. Cool and remove from baking pans. Use handle of wooden spoon to poke holes in first layer of cake; pour ½ pureed strawberries over layer. Set aside.

(Continued on next page.)

To prepare frosting, beat pudding mix and 1 cup skim milk in electric mixer on medium speed until well blended. Set aside. In separate bowl, combine Dream Whip, 1 cup cold skim milk, and 1 teaspoon vanilla. Beat on high speed for 4-6 minutes until peaks form. Fold mixture with pudding. Frost first layer of cake and add second layer. Make holes in second layer and pour remaining strawberries over second layer. Frost top and sides and garnish with fresh strawberries. Refrigerate at least 3 hours.

Yield: 16 servings
❦ *Calories: 285*
❦ *Fat: 4 grams*

Reduced Fat Pumpkin Cake

For a more economical recipe, make your own Streusel mix by crumbling brown sugar and cinnamon into a plain yellow cake mix. Try baking this cake in loaf pans and giving as holiday gifts!

1   box cinnamon Streusel coffee cake mix
1   cup water
½   cup applesauce
¾   cup fat free Egg Beaters
1   teaspoon cinnamon
¾   teaspoon pumpkin pie spice
1   cup pumpkin (or sweet potatoes), drained and mashed

Prepare cake mix according to directions on box, substituting applesauce and Egg Beaters for oil and eggs. Add spices and pumpkin and mix well. Bake at 350° for 35 minutes.

Yield: 16 servings
❦ *Calories: 215*
❦ *Fat: 5 grams*

Mardi Gras Cake

1   box yellow cake mix
1   small box sugar free instant vanilla pudding mix
1   cup fat free Egg Beaters
¾   cup water
¾   cup applesauce
1   teaspoon vanilla extract
1   teaspoon butter extract
¼   cup granulated sugar
¼   cup brown sugar
½   cup chopped nuts
1   teaspoon cinnamon

Glaze:

1   cup powdered sugar
1   teaspoon vanilla extract
1   teaspoon butter, melted
milk to desired consistency

Combine cake mix, pudding mix, Egg Beaters, water, applesauce, vanilla, and butter extract in mixing bowl and mix on medium speed for 8 minutes. In separate bowl, combine sugars, nuts, and cinnamon. Grease and flour a 9 × 13-inch pan. Pour ½ batter mixture into pan. Pour ½ sugar mixture over batter. Add remaining batter and top with remaining sugar. Swirl knife through batter. Bake at 350° for 40-45 minutes. Combine glaze ingredients and spread over cooled cake.

Yield: 12 servings
❦ *Calories: 220 (without glaze)*
❦ *Fat: 3 grams*

No Sugar Added Holiday Peppermint Cake

This recipe was demonstrated on my "Just Ask Stacey" cooking segment by Jonesboro, Louisiana native Selwyn Stewart, while she was a Nutrition and Dietetics student at Auburn University.

1 prepared angel food cake	1 teaspoon peppermint extract
3 cups sugar free vanilla ice cream, softened	1 (16-ounce) container fat free Cool Whip

Garnish:

20-25 small sugar free candy canes	Hershey's chocolate syrup
10 small sugar free candy canes, crushed	

Cut angel food cake in half and set aside top half. Combine ice cream and peppermint extract and spread over bottom half of cake and inside middle hole. Replace top half of cake. Spread Cool Whip over entire cake. Decorate sides of cake with small candy canes. Garnish top with crushed candy canes. Keep in freezer. Drizzle each slice with Hershey's syrup before serving.

Yield: 12 servings
❦ *Calories: 170 (without garnish)*
❦ *Fat: 2 grams*

Low Fat Chocolate Chip Pumpkin Cake

2	boxes reduced fat yellow cake mix	1	cup liquid Butter Buds
4	small boxes fat free instant chocolate pudding mix	2	cups water
		2	cups fat free Egg Beaters
		1	cup chocolate chips

Frosting:

	skim milk	1	ice cream cone (cake cup or sugar cone)
2	envelopes Dream Whip		
2	small boxes sugar free instant white chocolate pudding mix		green food color
			orange food color

Mix cake ingredients and pour into 2 Bundt pans sprayed with nonstick cooking spray. Bake at 325° for 45 minutes-1 hour or until toothpick inserted into center comes out clean. To make frosting, prepare Dream Whip and instant pudding using skim milk according to package directions; mix well. Set aside small amount of frosting (for pumpkin stem); add green food color and set aside. Add orange food color to remaining icing. Place 1 Bundt cake flat side up on cake platter; place other on top with flat sides together. Frost pumpkin with orange icing; place ice cream cone on top for stem, color with green icing. Decorate as desired.

Yield: 32 servings
❦ *Calories: 223 (with icing)*
❦ *Fat: 4¼ grams*

Easter Bonnet Cake

This cake is also great for showers and teas!

1 box yellow cake mix	8 ounces fat free
liquid Butter Buds	Cool Whip
fat free Egg Beaters	½ cup flaked coconut
1½ cups skim milk	
1 small box sugar free	
instant lemon	
pudding mix	

Garnish:

cloth ribbon	jelly beans
gum drops	silk flowers

Prepare cake mix according to package directions, substituting Butter Buds and Egg Beaters for oil and eggs. Pour batter into a greased and floured 1½-quart glass or metal oven-proof bowl. Pour remaining batter into a 12-inch round pizza pan. Bake at 350° for 15 minutes (pizza pan) and 45-50 minutes (bowl) or until toothpick inserted in center comes out clean.

(Continued on next page.)

Once cakes have cooled, turn the pizza pan cake onto a large serving tray and set aside. Remove bowl cake from bowl and split cake horizontally in half. Set aside. Pour milk into a small bowl and add pudding mix. Beat until blended. Set aside.

Spread the pizza pan cake with 1½ cups Cool Whip. Center bottom half (flat piece) of bowl cake on frosted pizza pan layer; spread ²/₃ cup pudding mixture on top of this layer. Add top layer of bowl cake.

Spread remaining whipped topping over cake. Sprinkle cake with coconut. Tie ribbon around cake crown to form a hat band and bow. Garnish with gum drops, jelly beans, flowers, etc.

Yield: 16 servings
❦ *Calories: 195 Calories*
❦ *Fat: 4 grams*

Low Fat Icebox Fruit Cake

As a child, I always looked forward to my mother making this treat at every Christmas.

1	package jumbo marshmallows (about 40)	3	tablespoons dry Butter Buds
¼	cup reduced fat margarine	¾	cup golden raisins
1	box graham cracker crumbs	½	cup raisins
		1	bottle maraschino cherries
		¼	cup chopped pecans

Melt margarine and marshmallows (add Butter Buds) in double boiler over medium heat, stirring to prevent burning. Combine crumbs and remaining ingredients. Add marshmallow mixture. Mix until well blended. Mold in foil pan or 2 small loaf pans. Refrigerate until cold.

Yield: 24 servings or 12 per loaf pan
❦ *Calories: 150*
❦ *Fat: 3 grams*

Easy Low Fat Cupcakes

1 box reduced fat
   yellow cake mix
3 tablespoons liquid
   Butter Buds

¾ cup fat free Egg
   Beaters
reduced fat frosting

Prepare cake mix according to directions on box, using Butter Buds and Egg Beaters. Frost each cupcake with 2 teaspoons reduced fat frosting.

Yield: 24 servings
❦ *Calories: 130*
❦ *Fat: 2 grams*

No Sugar Added Cheesecake

3 cups vanilla wafer crumbs

4 tablespoons margarine, melted

3 tablespoons sugar substitute

1 (¼-ounce) envelope unflavored gelatin

1 cup skim milk

2 (8-ounce) packages reduced fat cream cheese, softened

1 (3-ounce) package reduced fat cream cheese, softened

2 tablespoons lemon juice

1 tablespoon grated lemon rind

2 teaspoons vanilla extract

⅓-½ cup sugar substitute

Mix crumbs, margarine, and 3 tablespoons sugar substitute in medium bowl; pat evenly on bottom of 10 × 15-inch jelly roll pan. Sprinkle gelatin over milk in small saucepan; let stand 2-3 minutes. Heat over medium low heat, stirring constantly, until gelatin is dissolved. Cool to room temperature. Beat cream cheese until fluffy in large bowl; gradually beat in milk mixture. Beat in lemon juice and rind, vanilla, and ⅓ to ½ cup sugar substitute. Pour mixture over crust; refrigerate until set, about 3-4 hours. Garnish with fresh strawberries or fruit topping of your choice.

Yield: 16 servings
❦ *Calories: 145*
❦ *Fat: 2 grams*

Low Fat Caramel-Pecan Cheesecake

3 (8-ounce) packages fat free cream cheese
¾ cup granulated sugar
1 teaspoon vanilla extract
¾ cup fat free Egg Beaters
⅓ cup graham cracker crumbs
¼ cup chopped pecans
8 tablespoons caramel topping

Mix cream cheese, sugar, and vanilla with electric mixer on medium speed until well blended. Add Egg Beaters; mix just until blended. Spray 9-inch pie plate with nonstick cooking spray. Cover bottom of pan with graham cracker crumbs. Place pecans evenly over crumbs. Drizzle about 6-7 tablespoons of caramel topping over crust. Pour cream cheese mixture into pie plate. Bake at 325° for 45 minutes or until center is almost set. Cool. Refrigerate 3 hours or overnight. Drizzle remaining caramel on top before serving.

Yield: 10 servings
❧ *Calories: 230*
❧ *Fat: 3 grams*

Low Fat Mini Apple Pies

*Serve these pies with a scoop of my Fat Free
Homemade Ice Cream!*

1   cup apple pie filling
1   teaspoon cinnamon
1/8 teaspoon nutmeg
2   teaspoons
     granulated sugar
1   can low fat canned
     biscuits

flour
1   tablespoon reduced
     fat margarine, melted
2-3 tablespoons
     powdered sugar

In small bowl, mix pie filling, cinnamon, nutmeg, and sugar. Roll out each biscuit flat. Place small amount of mixture on one side of dough and fold over. Press sides with small amount of flour to close. Use knife to make 2-3 slits in top of pies. Brush small amount of melted margarine on top of each pie. Spray baking sheet with nonstick cooking spray; place pies on baking sheet. Bake at 450° for about 8 minutes. Allow to cool; dust each pie with powdered sugar before serving.

Yield: 10 servings
❦ *Calories: 90*
❦ *Fat: 1 gram*

Low Fat Double Berry Spoon Pie

3 cups fresh blueberries
3 cups fresh blackberries
1 tablespoon fresh lemon juice
8 tablespoons granulated sugar, divided
¼ cup plus 4 tablespoons all-purpose flour, divided
½ cup firmly packed brown sugar
½ teaspoon cinnamon
4 tablespoons reduced fat margarine, cut into small pieces
½ cup chopped pecans (optional)

Preheat oven to 375°. Combine blueberries, blackberries, lemon juice, 6 tablespoons sugar, and 2 tablespoons flour in a large bowl; transfer to a 2-quart shallow baking dish. Combine remaining flour and sugar, brown sugar, and cinnamon in medium bowl. With pastry blender or 2 knives, cut in margarine until crumbly. Stir in pecans, if desired. Sprinkle mixture evenly over fruit. Bake 10-15 minutes until top is brown and fruit is bubbly. Cool on wire rack. Serve warm or at room temperature with vanilla ice cream.

Yield: 12 servings
❦ *Calories: 140 (without pecans)*
❦ *Fat: 2 grams*

Low Fat Sugar Free Lemon Berry Pie

A sugar-free whipped topping, called "D'Zerta," is available in many stores. You may also use reduced fat Cool Whip.

4 ounces fat free cream cheese
1 tablespoon skim milk
1 tablespoon sugar substitute
1 tablespoon lemon juice
2 cups (4 envelopes) Dream Whip whipped topping, prepared according to directions
1 reduced fat graham cracker pie crust
1 pint strawberries, sliced
1 (4-ounce) box sugar free lemon instant pudding mix
2 cups skim milk

Beat cream cheese, milk, and sugar substitute in medium mixing bowl until smooth. Stir in lemon juice and 1 cup whipped topping. Spread evenly in graham cracker crust. Place sliced strawberries on top, reserving several for garnish. Prepare pudding using skim milk according to box directions. Let stand 1 minute and fold in 1 cup whipped topping. Spoon pudding mixture over strawberries. Refrigerate until set. Garnish with strawberries and additional whipped topping, if desired.

Yield: 8 servings
❧ *Calories: 160 (with crust)*
❧ *Fat: 3 grams*

Low Fat Lemon Icebox Pie

So easy, and so good!

1 egg yolk
1 can fat free sweetened condensed milk

¼ cup lemon juice
1 (6-ounce) reduced fat graham cracker pie crust

Meringue:

4 egg whites
¼ cup granulated sugar

pinch of cream tartar or salt

With spoon or spatula, fold egg yolk into sweetened condensed milk. Add lemon juice, folding until mixture is thickened. Pour mixture into pie crust. Beat egg whites with hand mixer. Add sugar and cream of tartar. Beat until peaks form. Spread meringue on pie and bake at 350° until brown. Refrigerate until set.

Yield: 8 servings
❦ *Calories: 275*
❦ *Fat: 3½ grams*

Reduced Fat Chilled Key Lime Pie

1 reduced fat graham cracker pie crust
1 can fat free sweetened condensed milk
¾ cup lime juice
½ cup fat free Egg Beaters
¼ teaspoon grated lime rind

1 envelope Dream Whip (2 cups prepared)
⅛ teaspoon green food color
1 envelope unflavored gelatin

Preheat oven to 350°. Bake pie crust 4-5 minutes or until lightly brown. Cool. In medium bowl, combine condensed milk, lime juice, Egg Beaters, and rind; whisk until well blended. Set aside. Mix Dream Whip according to package directions using skim milk. Fold prepared Dream Whip into condensed milk mixture; stir in food color. Prepare gelatin as directed on package, adding 1 cup boiling water to gelatin. Set aside or refrigerate to cool. Fold gelatin into filling and pour all into pie shell. Refrigerate 2-3 hours before serving.

Yield: 8 servings
❧ *Calories: 275*
❧ *Fat: 3½ grams*

No Sugar Added Lemon Ice Box Pie

Some of my television viewers have reported that the Crystal Light lemonade adds too much tartness. You may need to use only ½ package depending on your taste buds.

1 small box sugar free vanilla instant pudding mix
1¾ cups skim milk
1 tub Crystal Light lemonade powder (to make 2 quarts) or 1 package Kool Aid lemonade powder plus 1 cup sugar substitute

1 tablespoon lemon juice
8 ounces fat free Cool Whip
1 low fat graham cracker crust (See recipe in this book!)

Combine pudding and milk; add lemonade powder and lemon juice. Fold in ½ of the Cool Whip. Pour into crust and refrigerate until set. Top with Cool Whip.

Yield: 8 servings
❦ *Calories: 215*
❦ *Fat: 4 grams*

Reduced Fat Mom's Fresh Peach Pie

Crust:

1   package graham crackers, rolled fine (about 1²/₃ cups)

½   cup granulated sugar
¼   cup reduced fat margarine, softened

Filling:

1   cup granulated sugar
3   tablespoons cornstarch
1   cup water
4   tablespoons dry peach gelatin
½   cup granulated sugar

8   ounces light cream cheese
4-5 fresh peaches, peeled and sliced
Cool Whip

Prepare crust first by blending graham cracker crumbs with sugar and margarine. Press firmly against bottom and sides of a 9-inch pie plate. Bake at 375° for about 8 minutes. Set aside to cool. Combine 1 cup sugar, cornstarch, and water in a saucepan over high heat. Boil until thick and clear. Add gelatin. Set aside and let cool. Cream ½ cup sugar and cream cheese together until smooth and spread in bottom of cooled pie crust. Combine cooled gelatin mixture and peaches. Pour over cream cheese mixture. Cover with Cool Whip and refrigerate several hours or overnight before serving.

Yield: 12 servings
❧ *Calories: 200*

❦ *Fat: 3½ grams*

Reduced Fat Strawberry Cream Pie

1 (14-ounce) can fat free sweetened condensed milk
3 tablespoons lemon juice
8 ounces light Cool Whip

1½ pint fresh strawberries, sliced
2 (6-ounce) reduced fat graham cracker pie crusts

Mix lemon juice with sweetened condensed milk. Fold in Cool Whip. Add strawberries, folding until well blended. Pour ½ mixture into each crust.

Yield: 16 servings (8 per pie)
❦ *Calories: 215*

❦ *Fat: 4.75 grams*

Sugar Free Blueberry Pie

The filling for this pie is also fat free!

1	pound frozen blueberries	6	tablespoons water
½	teaspoon salt	¼	cup corn starch
½	teaspoon lemon juice	⅛	cup sugar substitute
¼	cup water	1	(9-inch) pie crust, baked and cooled

In medium saucepan, bring blueberries, salt, lemon juice and ¼ cup water to a boil. Mix 6 tablespoons water and ¼ corn starch and stir into boiling mixture until thickened. Remove from pan and cool to room temperature. Add sugar substitute to berries. Poor pie filling into crust.

Yield: 8 servings
❦ *Calories: 132*

❦ *Fat: 3½ grams*

Low Fat Louisiana Mud Pie

1 (7½-ounce) package reduced fat bite-sized chocolate chip cookies

3 tablespoons margarine, melted

2 cups fat free vanilla ice cream

½ envelope sugar free mocha cappuccino mix

1 cup miniature marshmallows

1 quart fat free chocolate ice cream

½ cup caramel sauce

Set aside 1 cup cookies; finely crush remaining cookies. In small bowl, combine cookie crumbs and margarine. Press mixture evenly on bottom of 9-inch pie plate. Chill 10 minutes. In medium bowl, combine 2 cups vanilla ice cream and ½ envelope cappuccino mix. Spread mixture on top of chilled crust. Top with reserved cookies and marshmallows. Scoop chocolate ice cream over cookie layer. Drizzle caramel sauce over ice cream. Freeze 4 hours or until firm.

Yield: 10 servings
❦ *Calories: 287*
❦ *Fat: 3.95 grams*

Reduced Fat and Calorie Pecan Pie

This was one of my most popular recipes ever! I hope you enjoy it as much as the television viewers did. It is a healthier version of the traditional favorite. Preparing it this way saves 210 calories and a whopping 15½ grams of fat per serving!

½ cup Egg Beaters	½ cup granulated sugar
2 tablespoons reduced fat margarine, melted	½ cup Karo syrup
	¼ cup boiling water
2 packages oatmeal (maple & brown sugar flavor)	½ cup chopped pecans
	1 (9-inch) pie shell

In large bowl, combine first 6 ingredients and mix well until blended. Add chopped pecans and pour into pie shell. Bake at 350° for about 45 minutes.

Yield: 10 servings
❦ *Calories: 240*
❦ *Fat: 9½ grams*

***Thanks to
Mr. T L Colvin, Sr. for sharing this exceptional recipe
with me, our viewers, and our readers.***

Reduced Fat Fresh Sweet Potato Pie

2 cups sweet potatoes
½ cup liquid Butter Buds
1 cup granulated sugar
1 cup fat free Egg Beaters
¾ can evaporated skim milk
1 teaspoon vanilla extract
1 teaspoon butter extract
½ teaspoon salt
½ teaspoon nutmeg
¼ teaspoon cloves
1 teaspoon cinnamon
2 (9-inch) pie shells, unbaked

Mix ingredients in order given. Pour into 2 unbaked pie shells. Bake at 450° for 25 minutes. Cover crust with foil to prevent burning.

Yield: 16 servings (8 servings per pie)
❦ *Calories: 165*
❦ *Fat: 4 grams*

No Sugar Added Double Layer Sweet Potato Pie

To make this recipe using sugar, use 1 tablespoon sugar for the 1½ packets of sugar substitute in cream cheese mixture.

4 ounces low fat cream cheese
1 tablespoon milk
1½ packets sugar substitute
12 ounces fat free Cool Whip
1 reduced fat graham cracker pie crust
1 cup skim milk
2 small boxes sugar free instant vanilla pudding mix
2 cups fresh cooked sweet potatoes, mashed
3½ teaspoons (12 packets) sugar substitute
1 teaspoon cinnamon
1 teaspoon vanilla extract
margarine

Mix cream cheese, 1 tablespoon milk, and 1½ packets sugar substitute in a large bowl with wire whisk until smooth. Gently stir in whipped topping. Spread on bottom of crust. Pour 1 cup skim milk into bowl. Add pudding mix. Beat until smooth. Mixture will be thick. Mix 12 packets sugar substitute or ½ cup sugar into sweet potatoes. Add cinnamon, vanilla, and a little margarine. Add to pudding mix. Spread over cream cheese layer. Refrigerate 3 hours. Garnish with additional Cool Whip.

Yield: 16 servings
❦ *Calories: 195*
❦ *Fat: 3 grams*

No Sugar Added Oreo Cookie Pie

6½ ounces sugar free chocolate sandwich cookies
¼ cup margarine, melted
8 ounces fat free cream cheese
½ cup sugar substitute
8 ounces fat free Cool Whip
1 small box sugar free instant chocolate pudding
1¾ cups skim milk

Crush cookies, reserving small amount for garnish. Mix cookies and melted margarine and press into 9-inch pie plate. Mix cream cheese, sugar substitute, and ½ container Cool Whip. Spread over cookies. Combine milk and pudding; pour over cream cheese mixture. Top with remaining Cool Whip. Sprinkle reserved cookie crumbs on top. Refrigerate.

Yield: 8 servings
❦ *Calories: 250*
❦ *Fat: 7 grams*

Low Fat Whippersnaps

*Lemon cake mix
works very well with this recipe.*

1	box cake mix with pudding	8	ounces light Cool Whip
1	teaspoon vanilla extract or flavoring of your choice	2	large egg whites
		¼	cup powdered sugar

Combine cake mix, vanilla, Cool Whip, and egg whites until thoroughly blended. Sift powdered sugar onto wax paper. Drop batter by teaspoons into powdered sugar and roll to coat. Place on cookie sheet prepared with nonstick cooking spray. Bake at 350° for about 10 minutes or until light brown. Do not overbake.

Yield: 4 dozen small cookies
❧ *Calories: 55*
❧ *Fat: less than one gram*

Stacey's Low Fat Oatmeal & Chocolate Chip Cookies

¾ cup applesauce
¾ cup brown sugar
1½ cups granulated
   sugar
3 teaspoons vanilla
   extract
6 egg whites

2 cups flour
1½ teaspoons salt
1½ teaspoons baking
   soda
3 cups oatmeal
1 cup chocolate chips

Beat applesauce, sugars, vanilla, and egg whites. Gradually add dry ingredients. Fold in oatmeal and chocolate chips. Bake at 350°.

Yield: 6 dozen
❦ *Calories: 65*
❦ *Fat: 1 gram*

Chocolate Chip Spider Web Cookie

This spooky treat is a hit at Halloween parties.
Just don't eat the spider!

1	box reduced fat yellow cake mix	1	teaspoon butter extract
4	egg whites	⅓	cup water
¼	cup liquid Butter Buds	¼	cup mini chocolate chips

To decorate:

1	container reduced fat vanilla frosting	low fat chocolate icing
		plastic spider

Preheat oven to 350°. Add liquid ingredients to ½ dry cake mix. Stir in remaining ingredients, except chocolate chips. Mix well. Do not overmix or cookie will be tough. Spread dough into round pizza pan sprayed with nonstick cooking spray. Sprinkle chocolate chips on top prior to baking. Bake 10-12 minutes and let cool. Frost with 1 container vanilla icing. Place 2-3 tablespoons low fat chocolate icing in plastic bag. Snip small hole in corner. Starting at outer edge, make continuous circle around pan, ending in the center. With a knife, start at center and pull out to make lines for web. Place plastic spider in center of web.

Yield: 24 servings
❦ *Calories: 150*
❦ *Fat: 2 grams*

Mardi Gras Cake Mix Cookies

1 box reduced fat yellow cake mix	2 tablespoons water
1 egg	nonstick cooking spray
1/3 cup applesauce	powdered sugar
1 teaspoon butter extract	colored sugar crystals or sprinkles (purple, yellow, green)

Preheat oven to 350°. Mix ingredients in mixing bowl. The dough should be stiff. Spray cookie sheet and hands with spray. Roll dough into small balls. Bake about 15 minutes until brown. Add water to powdered sugar to make a paste. Frost cookies with powdered sugar paste and sprinkle with sugar crystals or sprinkles.

Yield: 4 dozen
❦ *Calories: 43 (undecorated)*
❦ *Fat: ½ gram (undecorated)*

Light White Chocolate Chip and Cranberry Cookies

These festive cookies are great for holiday parties. Dry cranberries can be found in the self-serve bins in the produce section of large supermarkets.

½ cup margarine or butter, softened

1⅓ cups granulated sugar

½ cup fat free Egg Beaters or 2 eggs

1 teaspoon butter extract

1¾ cups all-purpose flour

1 cup rolled oats

1½ teaspoons baking soda

½ teaspoon salt

1 cup dried cranberries

⅔ cup white chocolate chips (vanilla milk chips)

Preheat oven to 350°. Spray cookie sheets with nonstick cooking spray. In large bowl, beat margarine and sugar until well blended. Add eggs and butter extract; mix well. Lightly spoon flour into measuring cup; level off. In small bowl, combine flour, rolled oats, baking soda, and salt. Stir into margarine mixture. Stir in cranberries and white chocolate chips. Drop by tablespoons 2 inches apart onto spray-coated cookie sheets. Bake at 350° for 9-11 minutes or until edges are golden brown. Cool 1 minute; remove from cookie sheets. Cool completely on wire racks. Store in tightly covered container.

Yield: 4 dozen cookies
❧ *Calories: 90*
❧ *Fat: 3 grams*

"Eggs in the Grass" Boiled Cookies

These cookies are a festive treat at Easter!

½ cup granulated sugar
⅓ cup reduced fat margarine
½ cup skim milk
⅓ cup reduced fat peanut butter
½ cup butterscotch chips
1 teaspoon vanilla extract
2 cups oatmeal (quick oats)
1½ cups chow mein noodles
green food color

Bring sugar, margarine, and milk to a rolling boil. Boil 4-5 minutes. Remove from heat; reduce heat to low or medium. Add peanut butter, butterscotch chips, and vanilla. Return to heat and stir until melted. Remove from heat; add oatmeal and chow mein noodles. Add green food color and spoon by teaspoons onto waxed paper. Press colored jelly beans into cookies for "eggs in the grass."

Yield: 4 dozen cookies
❦ *Calories: 50*
❦ *Fat: less than 2 grams*

Low Fat
French Vanilla Cookies

1   box French vanilla cake mix

½   cup fat free Egg Beaters

½   cup Smuckers Shortening & Oil Replacement or applesauce

¾   cup white chocolate chips

¼   cup chopped Macadamia nuts or pecans

Mix ingredients well until dough consistency. Drop by rounded teaspoons onto ungreased cookie sheet. Bake at 350° for about 10 minutes.

Yield: 4 dozen cookies
❦ *Calories: 75*
❦ *Fat: 2½ grams*

Sugar Free Raisin Bars

*These bars are great just out of the oven,
or chilled in the refrigerator.*

1 cup raisins
½ cup water
¼ cup margarine
1 teaspoon ground cinnamon
¼ teaspoon ground nutmeg
1 cup plain flour
1 egg, slightly beaten
¾ cup unsweetened applesauce
1 tablespoon sugar substitute
1 teaspoon baking soda
1 teaspoon vanilla extract
½ cup chopped nuts

In saucepan over medium heat, stir raisins, water, margarine, cinnamon, and nutmeg until margarine is melted; continue cooking for 3 minutes. Add all remaining ingredients. Spread into 8 × 8-inch dish prepared with nonstick cooking spray. Bake at 350° for 25-30 minutes or until lightly browned. Cut into squares.

Yield: 20 squares
❦ *Calories: 85*
❦ *Fat: 3 grams*

Low Fat Fudge Brownies

This was the first recipe I ever prepared on television—back in 1993! It was a hit then, and continues to be a hit today.

1 box fudge brownie mix	1 teaspoon vanilla extract
2 egg whites	1 teaspoon butter extract
⅓ cup plain nonfat yogurt or applesauce	3 tablespoons water

Preheat oven to 350°. Spray bottom of 9 × 13-inch pan with nonstick cooking spray. Empty brownie mix into large bowl; stir in remaining ingredients. Stir with spoon until well blended, about 50 strokes. Batter will be very thick. Spread batter into pan. Bake in center of oven about 25 minutes. Do not overbake. Cool completely before cutting.

Yield: 24 servings
❦ *Calories: 130*
❦ *Fat: 2 grams*

Low Fat Chess Squares

1 box reduced fat yellow cake mix	1 cup fat free Egg Beaters
½ cup liquid Butter Buds	8 ounces fat free cream cheese
2 tablespoons reduced fat margarine	1 teaspoon vanilla extract
4 cups powdered sugar	

Preheat oven to 350°. Combine cake mix, Butter Buds, and margarine and mix until well blended; batter will be very thick. Spread batter in baking pan sprayed with nonstick cooking spray. In separate bowl, combine powdered sugar, Egg Beaters, cream cheese, and vanilla; mix until well blended. Pour cream cheese mixture over batter. Bake at 350° for about 35 minutes. Cool and cut into small squares.

Yield: 5 dozen small squares
❦ *Calories: 75*
❦ *Fat: less than 1 gram*

Low Fat Hello Dollies

*This is such a rich treat that
no one will believe
it is low fat!*

3   tablespoons
    margarine
¼   cup liquid Butter
    Buds
1   cup graham cracker
    crumbs
1   cup miniature
    marshmallows

¼   cup shredded
    coconut
½   cup reduced fat
    chocolate chips
¼   cup pecans, chopped
1   can fat free
    sweetened
    condensed milk

Preheat oven to 350°. Using a 9 × 9-inch pan, melt margarine in pan, adding Butter Buds. Sprinkle graham cracker crumbs over margarine. Do not stir ingredients at any time. Layer marshmallows and shredded coconut. Sprinkle chocolate chips over coconut. Add pecans; then pour canned milk over entire mixture. Cover pan with foil and bake 30 minutes. Cool; then cut into squares.

Yield: 24 servings
❦ *Calories: 105*
❦ *Fat: 3 grams*

Low Fat Triple Chocolate Valentine Brownies

It wouldn't be Valentine's Day without chocolate.
Now you can enjoy a delicious chocolate treat
with your sweetheart — without the guilt!

1¼ cups unsifted flour
¼ cup granulated sugar
⅓ cup margarine, melted
1 (14-ounce) can fat free sweetened condensed milk
¼ cup unsweetened cocoa

1 egg
1 teaspoon vanilla extract
½ teaspoon baking powder
⅓ cup reduced fat chocolate chips

Preheat oven to 350°. Line 9 × 13-inch baking pan with aluminum foil; set aside. In mixing bowl, combine 1 cup flour and sugar; add melted margarine. Press on bottom of pan. Bake 15 minutes. In separate bowl, beat condensed milk, cocoa, egg, remaining ¼ cup flour, vanilla, and baking powder. Stir in chocolate chips. Spread over prepared crust. Bake 20 minutes or until set. Cool. Use foil to lift out of pan. Cut with heart-shaped cookie cutter or, with knife, cut around waxed paper heart shape. Decorate with icing or gels if desired. Store in covered container.

Yield: 16 servings
❦ *Calories: 160*
❦ *Fat: 3 grams*

Low Fat Cappuccino Fudge Brownie (Pumpkin Patch Brownie, Spider Web, & Spooky Spiders)

1 box supreme brownie mix with syrup pouch
½ cup applesauce or ½ cup plain fat free yogurt
½ cup fat free Egg Beaters
¼ cup hot cappuccino

Heat oven to 350°. Prepare brownie mix according to box directions, substituting applesauce and Egg Beaters for oil and eggs. Add hot cappuccino and mix well.

Pumpkin Patch Brownie:

Bake mix in 9 × 13-inch pan. Allow to cool; frost with reduced fat vanilla frosting. Cut into 18 squares. Place candy pumpkin in center of each brownie and pipe green frosting to make a vine and leaf design on each square.

(Continued on next page.)

Spider Web:

Bake mix in round pizza pan. Allow to cool. Fill a cake decorating bag with reduced fat vanilla frosting and pipe concentric circles on cookie, starting from outer edge to inside. Use a knife to pull from center to outer edge to make web.

Spooky Spiders:

Bake about 1½ tablespoons batter in each cup of a muffin top pan. Allow to cool; frost with reduced fat chocolate frosting. Use 2 Red Hots candies for eyes and make 6 small legs out of licorice sticks.

Yield: about 18 servings
❦ *Calories: 140 (undecorated)*
❦ *Fat: 1½ -2 grams*

Low Fat Butterscotch Chocolate Chip Bars

1 box reduced fat yellow cake mix

1 small box butterscotch instant pudding mix

½ cup fat free Egg Beaters

½ cup liquid Butter Buds

¼ cup brown sugar

1 teaspoon butter extract

⅓ cup skim milk (may use less; add as needed)

¾ cup reduced fat semisweet chocolate chips

Preheat oven to 375°. Spray 9 × 13-inch pan with nonstick cooking spray. Combine cake mix, dry pudding mix, Egg Beaters, liquid Butter Buds, brown sugar, and butter extract in large bowl. Mix with spoon until blended, adding skim milk as needed. Spread in pan. Bake 20-25 minutes. Do not over bake. Cut into bars before serving.

Yield: 24 bars
❦ *Calories: 135*
❦ *Fat: 2 grams*

Christmas in a Jar
White Christmas Bars

½ cup white chocolate or vanilla milk chips

⅓ cup slices almonds, toasted

½ cup packed light brown sugar

1 cup reduced fat buttermilk biscuit and baking mix

½ cup packed dark brown sugar

1 cup reduced fat buttermilk biscuit and baking mix

In a 1-quart wide-mouthed glass jar, gently layer and pack ingredients in the order listed, beginning with the white chocolate chips. If there is any space left after adding the last ingredient, add more white chocolate chips to fill the jar. Place lid on top. Cut an 8-inch circle of fabric to cover lid. Place fabric over lid; secure in place with ribbon or raffia. Decorate as desired.

Attach a gift card that reads:

"White Christmas Bars"

Empty contents of jar into a medium bowl. Stir in ¼ cup margarine and ¼ cup applesauce, 1 egg, and 1 teaspoon vanilla extract. Press into an 8 × 8-inch baking pan coated with nonstick cooking spray. Bake at 350° for 25 minutes. Makes 16 bars.

Yield: 16 bars (prepared)
❦ *Calories: 145*
❦ *Fat: 5 grams*

I Can't Believe It's Low Fat Homemade Ice Cream (with Real Candy Bars!)

1   cup fat free Egg Beaters
1   teaspoon salt
1½ cups granulated sugar
2   (12-ounce) cans evaporated skim milk
1   (14-ounce) can low fat sweetened condensed milk

2   teaspoons vanilla extract
6   cups skim milk (or to fill line)
4   Three Musketeers candy bars, frozen

Beat Egg Beaters with electric mixer until fluffy. Beat in salt and sugar. Add evaporated skim milk, sweetened condensed milk, and vanilla. Mix well and pour into ice cream freezer; add skim milk until mixture reaches fill line. Stir mixture well. Chop frozen candy bars into very small pieces or chips; add to ice cream mixture. Freeze with homemade ice cream freezer until firm.

Yield: 16 servings
❦ *Calories: 250*
❦ *Fat: 3 grams*

Stacey's Fat Free No Sugar Added Homemade Ice Cream

2   envelopes unflavored gelatin
2   cans evaporated skim milk
¾ cup Egg Beaters

1½ cups sugar substitute (or 1½ cups granulated sugar)
1   tablespoon vanilla extract
3   cups skim milk

In a medium saucepan, combine gelatin and 2 cans milk. Let stand 5 minutes. Cook and stir over medium heat until mixture comes to a boil and gelatin is dissolved. In mixing bowl, combine Egg Beaters and sugar substitute and cream together on medium speed. Add vanilla and 1½ cups skim milk. Pour gelatin mixture into sugar mixture. Chill completed mixture until cool. Freeze according to directions in a 4-quart electric ice cream freezer. Add 1½ cups skim milk or enough to fill to proper level before starting ice cream freezer.

Yield: 14 servings
❦ *Calories: 130*
❦ *Fat: 0 grams*

No Sugar Added Fat Free Sweet Potato Ice Cream

1¾ cups fat free Egg Beaters

2¾ cups sugar substitute

1 (13-ounce) can fat free evaporated skim milk

2 (14-ounce) cans fat free sweetened condensed milk

1½ teaspoon vanilla extract

3 cups sweet potatoes, cooked, drained, and creamed

8 cups skim milk or enough to fill ice cream freezer

Beat Egg Beaters until stiff. Add remaining ingredients slowly, beating mixture after each addition. Pour mixture into ice cream freezer container; add milk until mixture reaches fill line.

Yield: about 24 servings
❦ *Calories: 160*
❦ *Fat 0 grams*

Fat Free Easy Ice Cream

1 large box fat free
 sugar free vanilla
 instant pudding mix
1½ cups granulated
 sugar
4 cups skim milk
1 large can evaporated
 skim milk
1 cup water

1 teaspoon vanilla
 extract
1 can fat free
 sweetened
 condensed milk
20 miniature Milky
 Way Lite candy
 bars, cut up

Stir above ingredients and pour into ice cream freezer. Finish filling freezer with skim milk.

Yield: 16 servings
❦ *Calories: 225 (188 without candy)*
❦ *Fat: 1 gram (0 without candy)*

Reduced Fat Blueberry Delight

2 cups graham cracker crumbs
½ cup sifted powdered sugar
¼ cup finely chopped pecans
¼ cup reduced fat margarine, melted
8 ounces fat free cream cheese
¾ cup granulated sugar
½ cup fat free Egg Beaters
½ cup low fat sweetened condensed milk
2 tablespoons lemon juice
2 cups light blueberry filling
light Cool Whip

Preheat oven to 350°. Combine first three ingredients; add melted margarine, stirring well. Spray 9 × 13-inch baking pan with nonstick cooking spray and press graham cracker mixture into pan. Beat cream cheese at medium speed with electric mixer until smooth. Add sugar, Egg Beaters, milk, and lemon juice, mixing until smooth. Spread over crust. Bake at 350° for 20-25 minutes or until set. Cool completely. Spread pie filling over cream cheese mixture. Cover and refrigerate several hours. Top each serving with 1 tablespoon light Cool Whip.

Yield: 16 servings
❦ *Calories: 278*
❦ *Fat: 4 grams*

Easy Low Fat Blueberry Cobbler

This recipe works well with any fruit!

½ cup reduced fat
    margarine, melted
1 cup flour
1 cup granulated
    sugar
1 cup skim milk

1 teaspoon baking
    powder
3 cups blueberries
    (fresh, frozen,
    or canned)

Pour melted margarine in bottom of rectangular cake pan. In mixing bowl, combine flour, sugar, and milk. Mix until well blended and pour evenly over margarine. Spread blueberries over batter. Bake at 350° for 45 minutes or until golden brown.

Yield: 12 servings
❦ *Calories: 150*
❦ *Fat: 3 grams*

Fat Free Lemon Mousse

You may use an additional container of fat free Cool Whip to layer this recipe.

2   egg yolks, beaten
1   can fat free
     sweetened
     condensed milk
⅓   cup fresh squeezed
     lemon juice

8   ounces fat free Cool
     Whip
fresh lemon peel, grated

Add sweetened condensed milk to beaten eggs; stir in lemon juice until well blended. Fold in Cool Whip. Add lemon peel to increase flavor.

Yield: 10 servings of about ½ cup each
❦ *Calories: 165*
❦ *Fat: less than 1 gram*

Low Fat Banana Pudding

32 vanilla wafers
4 bananas
1 large box fat free
   sugar free vanilla
   pudding

3 cups skim milk
1 cup fat free sour
   cream
8 ounces light
   Cool Whip

Line bottom of medium dish with 16 vanilla wafers. Slice 2 bananas and place slices over wafers. Prepare pudding with skim milk as directed on package. Add 1 cup sour cream and 1 cup Cool Whip to pudding mixture. Pour mixture over wafers and bananas. Slice remaining 2 bananas over pudding mixture. Use remaining Cool Whip for top layer. Place wafers around edge or as desired.

Yield: 10 servings
❧ *Calories: 170*
❧ *Fat: 1.5 grams*

Low Fat Turtle Trifle

1   (22½-ounce) package supreme brownie mix with hot fudge pouch
1   large (2.1-ounce) box sugar free instant chocolate pudding mix

12 ounces fat free Cool Whip, thawed
2   small (snack size) reduced fat candy bars (chocolate toffee crisp bars), chopped caramel ice cream topping

Bake brownies according to package directions, substituting applesauce for oil. Cool and crumble into casserole or serving dish. Prepare pudding according to box directions, using skim milk. Sprinkle ⅓ crumbled brownies in dish; top with ⅓ pudding mixture. Spread with ⅓ Cool Whip. Repeat layers twice. Sprinkle with chopped candy bars and garnish with caramel topping. Cover and chill 6 hours.

Yield: 24 servings
❦ *Calories: 150 (without garnish)*
❦ *Fat: 2 grams*

Low Fat Four Layer Delight

First Layer:

1 cup flour
4 tablespoons low fat margarine

2 tablespoons fat free margarine
1 teaspoon butter extract
1/3 cup pecans, chopped

Second Layer:

4 ounces fat free cream cheese
4 ounces low fat cream cheese

1 cup powdered sugar
8 ounces fat free Cool Whip

Third Layer:

1 large box sugar free instant chocolate pudding mix

3 cups skim milk

Fourth Layer:

fat free Cool Whip (remaining from 8-ounce container)

Mix First Layer ingredients and press into a rectangle baking dish. Bake at 350° about 20-25 minutes until brown. Cool completely. For Second Layer, blend cream cheese and sugar; fold in Cool Whip. Spread over cooled crust. Prepare Third Layer by mixing pudding with milk. Pour over cream cheese layer. For Fourth Layer, spread remaining Cool Whip over chocolate pudding mixture.

Yield: 16
❦ *Calories: 165*
❦ *Fat: 5 grams*

Low Fat Hawaiian Delight

This recipe is great for a Hawaiian luau or any summer "get-together." I prepare it in a palm tree-shaped dish to add a festive look.

32 reduced fat vanilla
   wafers
8 ounces fat free cream
   cheese, softened
1 (14-ounce) can
   fat free sweetened
   condensed milk
2 tablespoons lemon
   juice
1 (15-ounce) can
   crushed pineapple in
   its own juice, drained

2 medium bananas,
   sliced
1 (13½-ounce)
   container fat free
   Cool Whip
Shredded coconut and
   Maraschino
   cherries for garnish

Line bottom of 9 × 13-inch dish with wafers. Use remaining wafers to line sides of dish. Mix cream cheese, condensed milk, and lemon juice with mixer until smooth. Spread over vanilla wafer crust. Chill 30 minutes. Spread pineapple over filling and top with sliced bananas. Cover with Cool Whip. Garnish with coconut and cherries. Chill well before serving.

Yield: 16 servings
❣ *Calories: 200*
❣ *Fat: 1½ grams*

No Sugar Added Fresh Tropical Fruit Trifle

Be creative with this dessert. Try using pineapple, strawberries, grapes, cantaloupe, honey dew, kiwi, bananas, peaches, berries, and more! You'll enjoy finding the combination your family likes best.

1 large box sugar free vanilla instant pudding mix	4 cups mixed fresh fruit (or canned fruit in its own juice)
1 teaspoon coconut extract	¼ cup sugar substitute
1 tablespoon pineapple juice	¼ cup shredded coconut
1 cup fat free sour cream	1 large prepared angel food cake

Prepare pudding according to directions on box, using skim milk. Add coconut extract, pineapple juice, and sour cream. Combine sugar substitute and coconut with fruit; toss. Tear angel food cake into small pieces. Layer the cake, fruit, and pudding ½ portion at a time in a large trifle bowl. Garnish with fresh fruit. Chill, covered, at least 2 hours before serving.

Yield: 20 servings
❦ *Calories: 115*
❦ *Fat: less than 1 gram*

No Sugar Added Strawberry Trifle

1 small box sugar free strawberry gelatin
2 cups frozen sliced strawberries (no sugar added)
8 ounces fat free cream cheese, softened

1 cup sugar substitute
12 ounces fat free Cool Whip
1 prepared angel food cake, broken into small pieces

Dissolve gelatin in 1 cup boiling water. Divide gelatin into two bowls, with ½ cup in each bowl. Place 1 cup sliced strawberries in each bowl. Stir and set aside. Cream softened cream cheese and artificial sweetener. Fold in Cool Whip. In trifle or serving bowl, layer cake, strawberry mixture, and cream cheese mixture until all ingredients are used, finishing with cream cheese mixture.

Yield: 16 servings
❦ *Calories: 185*
❦ *Fat: 0 grams*

Quick and Easy Low Fat Strawberry Trifle Delight

I prepare this recipe using Marie's Strawberry Glaze, found in the produce section of the supermarket, and fresh Louisiana strawberries!

1	prepared angel food cake	1	(14-ounce) container strawberry glaze
1	large carton strawberries, sliced	1	large container light Cool Whip

Tear cake into pieces and line bottom of trifle bowl. Combine strawberries and glaze. Spread over cake layer. Top strawberry mixture with Cool Whip. Continue the three layers (cake, strawberries, Cool Whip) using all of cake and strawberries. Top with remaining Cool Whip.

Yield: 24 servings
❦ *Calories: 140*
❦ *Fat: less than 1 gram*

Low Fat Fruit Pizza

1 box sugar cookie mix
¼ cup liquid Butter Buds
½ teaspoon butter extract
8 ounces fat free cream cheese, softened
⅓ cup powdered sugar

½ teaspoon vanilla extract
Fresh fruit (strawberries, blueberries, bananas, pineapple, grapes, peaches) or canned fruit in its own juice

Glaze:

⅔ cup granulated sugar
2 tablespoons cornstarch

¼ teaspoon salt
1 cup orange juice

Prepare cookie mix according to box directions for *rolled* cookies, replacing oil with Butter Buds. Add butter extract. Press in the bottom of a pizza pan to form crust. Bake at 375° for 8 minutes or 350° for 12 minutes until golden brown. Mix cream cheese, powdered sugar, and vanilla and spread onto cooled cookie crust. Combine glaze ingredients in saucepan and boil one minute *only*, stirring continuously. Cool at least 5 minutes. Arrange fresh fruit on cookie crust and cover completely with glaze. Refrigerate overnight before serving.

Yield: 24 servings
❧ *Calories: 150 (does not include calories from fruit)*
❧ *Fat: 3 grams*

Low Fat Halloween Trifle

2   boxes low fat
    chocolate cream
    cookies
2   small boxes fat free
    vanilla instant
    pudding mix

4   cups skim milk
    yellow and red (or
    orange) food color
12 ounces light Cool
    Whip

Decorate:

vanilla cream-filled
    cookies (rectangle-
    shaped)

candy corn &
    pumpkins

Using food processor or chopper, make cookie crumbs with cookies. Set aside. Prepare pudding with skim milk according to box directions and use food coloring to make pudding orange. Set aside. Spread ⅓ cookie crumbs in bottom of trifle dish, covering completely. Pour ½ pudding mixture over cookie crumbs. Place ⅓ Cool Whip on top. Continue to layer, ending with Cool Whip and garnishing with cookie crumbs. Decorate as a graveyard, using candy corn and pumpkins, and vanilla cookies as tombstones.

Yield: 32 servings
❧ *Calories: 130*
❧ *Fat: 2.5*

Witches Hands

*Let your children or grandchildren
help prepare this fat free snack!*

12 clear plastic gloves   60 pieces candy corn
18 cups fat free
   caramel popcorn

Place one candy corn in each finger of each glove.
Fill gloves with 1½ cup popcorn. Tie with bow.

Yield: 12 servings
❦ *Calories: 200*
❦ *Fat: 0 grams*

Low Fat Pumpkin Roll

½ cup pumpkin	1 teaspoon baking soda
1 cup granulated sugar	½ teaspoon cinnamon
¾ cup fat free Egg Beaters	dash nutmeg
	¾ cup flour

Filling:

2 tablespoons margarine	1 cup powdered sugar
8 ounces light cream cheese	¾ teaspoon vanilla extract

Mix all ingredients together until well blended. Spray cookie sheet or jelly roll pan with nonstick cooking spray; line with wax paper that has also been prepared with nonstick spray. Pour mixture onto wax paper and bake at 350° for 15 minutes. Remove from oven and turn onto a dish towel dusted with powdered sugar. Roll mixture (with wax paper) tightly and place in refrigerator for 2 hours. Remove, unroll and spread with cream cheese filling. Re-roll. Refrigerate before serving.

Yield: 16 servings
❧ *Calories: 150*
❧ *Fat: 4 grams*

Pumpkin Trifle

If pumpkin pie spice is not available,
use ¼ teaspoon ground nutmeg,
¼ teaspoon ground ginger,
and ¼ teaspoon ground allspice.

1   box spice cake mix
fat free Egg Beaters
cinnamon applesauce
1   (16-ounce) can
    pumpkin or sweet
    potatoes, drained
1   teaspoon ground
    cinnamon
¾   teaspoon pumpkin
    pie spice

2½ cups cold milk
4   small boxes sugar
    free instant vanilla
    pudding mix
8   ounces light Cool
    Whip
maraschino cherries
    (optional) candy corn
    or pumpkins to
    decorate (optional)

(Continued on next page.)

Prepare spice cake mix according to directions on box; substituting Egg Beaters for eggs and cinnamon applesauce for oil. After cake has cooled, crumble cake and set aside ¼ cup for topping. Divide remaining crumbs into four portions and sprinkle one portion into bottom of trifle or 3-quart serving bowl. In a large mixing bowl, combine pumpkin or sweet potato, spices, milk, and pudding mix; mix until smooth. Spoon half of mixture into serving bowl. Sprinkle with second portion of crumbs. Spoon half of the Cool Whip into bowl, and sprinkle with third portion of crumbs. Top with the remaining pumpkin or sweet potato mixture. Add fourth portion of crumbs and remaining Cool Whip. Sprinkle reserved crumbs on top and around sides of bowl. Place cherries in center and decorate as desired. Cover and chill at least 2 hours before serving.

Yield: 24 servings
❦ *Calories: 160*
❦ *Fat: 3 grams*

Low Fat Spooky Graveyard Treat

2   cups (1 box) low fat
     chocolate cream
     cookies, finely crushed
nonstick cooking spray
8   ounces fat free
     cream cheese
¼   cup granulated sugar
1   container light
     Cool Whip

1   large box sugar free
     vanilla pudding mix
3   cups skim milk
1   teaspoon butter
     extract
yellow and red food
     color

Decorations:

low fat cream-filled
     sandwich cookies
     (rectangle-shaped)

candy corn & pumpkins

Spread cookie crumbs (about 1 cup) on bottom of 9 × 13-inch dish until covered well. Spray crumbs with nonstick cooking spray and press firmly. Beat cream cheese and ¼ cup sugar until smooth; fold in 1 cup Cool Whip. Spoon cream cheese mixture over cookie crumbs. Mix pudding according to directions, using 3 cups skim milk. Add 1 teaspoon butter flavoring and yellow and red food color to make pudding orange. Spoon pudding mixture over cream cheese mixture. Refrigerate 2-3 hours or until firm. Spread remaining Cool Whip over pudding layer. Sprinkle with remaining cookie crumbs. Decorate as a graveyard for Halloween.

Yield: 16 servings
❦ *Calories: 140 (undecorated)*
❦ *Fat: 3 grams*

Reduced Fat Spring Four-Layer Delight

1 cup flour
½ cup reduced fat margarine
¼ cup pecans
8 ounces fat free cream cheese
1 cup fat free Cool Whip
1 cup powdered sugar

1 large box sugar free instant white chocolate pudding mix
3 cups skim milk
green food color
red food color
toasted coconut to decorate

Combine flour, margarine, and pecans and bake in 9 × 11-inch pan at 375° for 20 minutes. Mix cream cheese, Cool Whip, and powdered sugar and pour over first layer. Combine pudding mix and milk and divide in half. Add 1 drop green food color to ½ pudding mixture and pour over cream cheese mixture. Add 1 drop red food color to other ½ pudding mixture and pour over green layer. Repeat green and pink layers until gone. Spread additional Cool Whip over top and sprinkle with toasted coconut or decorate as desired.

Yield: 16 servings
❦ *Calories: 190*
❦ *Fat: 4 grams*

Reduced Fat "Reindeer Food"

These nibblers are so good that you'll want to keep eating, but remember that those little handfuls add up! Place some "Reindeer Food" in pretty containers and give as gifts. That way you can spread the Christmas Spirit and the Christmas Calories; and not have them all for yourself! Let children help in the easy preparation and don't forget to let them leave some outside for Santa's Reindeer on Christmas Eve!

9   squares vanilla candy coating (Almond Bark)
3   cups mini pretzels
½   cup cocktail peanuts
3   cups small marshmallows (optional)
6½ cups frosted toasted O-shaped cereal
5½ cups crisp rice cereal squares
1   cup red & green candy coated chocolate pieces

Place candy coating in a microwave safe container and microwave on high 3 minutes or until melted, stirring every 30-60 seconds. Combine pretzels, peanuts, marshmallows, and cereals in a large bowl; pour melted candy coating over mixture, tossing to coat. Stir in chocolate pieces. Spread mixture onto wax paper. Let stand 30 minutes. Break into pieces and store in airtight container.

Yield: 65 servings of ⅓ cup each
❦ *Calories: 75*
❦ *Fat: 3 grams*

Low Fat Cranberry Fluff

2 cups fresh cranberries, finely chopped
3 cups miniature marshmallows
½ cup granulated sugar
2 cups Red Delicious apples, diced
½ cup red or white grapes, sliced
¼ cup pecans, chopped
¼ teaspoon salt
8 ounces fat free Cool Whip

Mix together cranberries, marshmallows, and sugar and chill overnight. Fold remaining ingredients into chilled cranberry mixture.

Yield: 15 servings
❦ *Calories: 125*
❦ *Fat: 1 gram*

Low Fat Christmas Bread Pudding

1 cup evaporated skim milk	2 tablespoons raisins
½ cup low fat sweetened condensed milk	¼ teaspoon ground nutmeg
1 egg	¼ teaspoon vanilla extract
4 slices stale bread (40 calories per slice), cut into ½-inch cubes	⅛ teaspoon ground cinnamon
3 tablespoons granulated sugar	1 tablespoon reduced fat margarine

Preheat oven to 375°. In a medium bowl, beat together milk and egg. Add the bread cubes and let soak for 30 minutes. Stir in 3 tablespoons sugar, raisins, nutmeg, vanilla, and cinnamon, mixing well. Spoon the mixture in an 8-inch square baking dish prepared with nonstick vegetable cooking spray. Dot with the margarine and bake for 30 minutes or until firm. Top with Rum Sauce.

Yield: 6 servings
❧ *Calories: 180 (without sauce)*
❧ *Fat: 2 grams*

Rum or Whiskey Sauce

1 small box vanilla pudding (not instant)
2²/₃ cups milk

1 teaspoon nutmeg
1 jigger whiskey or 1 teaspoon rum extract

Heat pudding and milk over low to medium heat. Add nutmeg. Allow pudding to thicken, about 15-20 minutes. Add flavoring.

Fat Free Rice Krispies Holiday Treats

1 teaspoon butter extract
3 tablespoons dry Butter Buds

40 large marshmallows or 4 cups miniature marshmallows
6 cups Holiday Rice Krispies

Spray saucepan with nonstick cooking spray. Add marshmallows and stir over low heat until completely melted. Add Butter Buds and butter extract; stir until well blended. Remove from heat; add Rice Krispies. Stir until well coated. Spray 9 × 13-inch pan and a spatula with nonstick cooking spray and spread cereal mixture into pan. Cool; cut into squares.

Yield: 24 treats (2 × 2-inches)
❦ *Calories: 63*
❦ *Fat: 0 grams*

Cinnamon Bread Pudding
with Whiskey Sauce

5   cups cinnamon bread pieces (1-inch cubes)
¼   cup raisins or dried currants
2   eggs
2   egg whites
¾   cup granulated sugar
2½ cups hot skim milk

Whiskey Sauce:

1   cup granulated sugar
1   cup water
¼   cup whiskey (or ¼ cup water and 1 teaspoon brandy extract)
¼   cup nonfat vanilla yogurt

Heat oven to 375°. Spray a 9 × 13-inch baking dish with nonstick cooking spray. Combine bread cubes and raisins in dish. In medium bowl, combine eggs, egg whites, and ¾ cup sugar; beat well. Add hot milk and mix well. Pour mixture over bread and raisins; let stand 5 minutes. Stir gently. Bake at 375° for 25-35 minutes or until liquid is absorbed. Meanwhile, in small saucepan, combine 1 cup sugar and water; mix well. Bring to a boil; boil 5 minutes. Remove from heat and stir in whiskey. Cool to lukewarm. Stir in yogurt. Serve warm bread pudding with warm sauce.

Yield: 8 servings
❧ *Calories: 330*
❧ *Fat: 3 grams*

Fat Free
Cherries in the Snow

1   cup granulated sugar
8   ounces fat free
    cream cheese
½   cup skim milk
12 ounces fat free
    Cool Whip

1   (8-ounce) prepared
    angel food cake
1   can light cherry pie
    filling
cherries for garnish

Cream together sugar, cream cheese, and milk. Fold in Cool Whip. Place thin slices or pieces of angel food cake in bottom of trifle dish. Spoon cream cheese mixture over cake. Spoon pie filling over cream cheese mixture. Continue layering until all ingredients are used, ending with cream cheese. Garnish with cherries.

Yield: 20 servings
❦ *Calories: 130*
❦ *Fat: 0 grams*

Low Fat Graham Cracker Crust

Reduce the fat and calorie content of your recipes by making your own graham cracker crusts! You may find that 1 cup of crushed graham crackers is sufficient for a small pie.

1½ cups crushed graham crackers (about 8 full-sized crackers)
2   tablespoons sugar substitute or 1 tablespoon granulated sugar

2   tablespoons liquid Butter Buds

Place all ingredients in small mixing bowl and mix with a fork until moistened. Press into 8 or 9-inch pie pan prepared with nonstick cooking spray.

Yield: 8 servings
❦ *Calories: 40*
❦ *Fat: 1 gram*

INDEX

A

After School Snacks
Bugs on a Log 62
Peanut Butter Squares 62
Pizza Squares 63

Almond Tea 69

Appetizers
Fat Free Chicken Enchilada
Dip 40
Fat Free Corn Dip 41
Fat Free Spectacular Spinach
Dip 42
Low Fat Creamy Artichoke
and Broccoli Dip 43
Low Fat Dip Chips 44
Low Fat Seven-Layer Tex
Mex Dip 45
Reduced Fat Cheesy Chili
Dip 46
Reduced Fat Cheesy
Crawfish Dip 47
Reduced Fat Hot Seafood
Dip 48
Reduced Fat Cajun Shrimp
Dip 49
Christmas In a Jar Mexican
Dip Mix 50
Catfish Party Dip 51
Fat Free Easy Shrimp Dip
52
Nantucket Crab 53
Low Fat Ham Roll Ups
53
Low Fat Spicy Chicken
Quesadillas 54

Fat Free Tortilla Roll Ups
55
Low Fat Ham Delights 56
Fat Free Nibblers 57
Low Fat Veggie Bars 58
Yogurt Fruit Dressing 59
Fat Free Crabmeat Surprise
Tray 60
Low Fat Ham & Cheese
Biscuits 61

Apples
Fat Free Harvest Apple
Muffins 116
Low Fat Apple Spice Cake
207

B

Bars
Sugar Free Raisin Bars
267
Low Fat Fudge Brownies
268
Low Fat Chess Squares
269
Low Fat Hello Dollies 270
Low Fat Triple Chocolate
Valentine Brownies 271
Low Fat Cappuccino Fudge
Brownie (Pumpkin Patch
Brownie, Spider Web &
Spooky Spiders) 272
Low Fat Butterscotch
Chocolate Chip Bars
274
Christmas in a Jar White
Christmas Bars 275

Beef
Reduced fat Mexican
Lasagna 159
Reduced Fat Tater Tot
Casserole 160
Low Fat Hot Tamale Pie 161
Low Fat Baked Cabbage
Jambalaya 162
Reduced Fat Slow Cooker
Lasagna 163
Reduced Fat Meat and
Cheese Pistolettes 164
Reduced Fat Pizza Pie 165
Reduced Fat Crescent Pizza
Pie 166
Reduced Fat Chuck Wagon
Chili Casserole 167
Reduced Fat Chili Spaghetti
168
Reduced Fat Chili Bake
169
Reduced Fat Cabbage Roll
Casserole 170
Reduced Fat Beef & Salsa
Burritos 171
Low Fat Speedy Taco bake
172
Low Fat Lasagna 173
Beef Noodle Casserole 174
Low Fat Oven Stew 175
Light Filet Mignon 176
Beef & Chicken Kabobs
177

Beef Noodle Casserole 174
Best Ever Low Fat Baked
Chicken 148

Beverages
Red Hot Punch 64

Christmas In a Jar Sugar
Free Spiced Tea 65
Christmas In a Jar Hot
Chocolate Mix 66
Fat Free Wassil 63
Sugar Free Punch 67
Strawberry Yogurt Smoothie
68
Almond Tea 69

Blueberries
Modified Blueberry Salad
102
Low Fat Double Berry
Spoon Pie 247
Sugar Free Blueberry Pie
254
Easy Low Fat Blueberry
Cobbler 281

Breads
Low Fat Cornbread
Dressing 110
Stacey's Fat Free Mexican
Cornbread 111
Fat Free Banana Bread
112
Low Fat Hawaiian Bread
113
Low Fat Cheesy Seafood
Bread 114
Low Fat Spicy Apple
Muffins 115
Fat Free Harvest Apple
Muffins 116

Broccoli
Low Fat Creamy Artichoke
and Broccoli Dip 43
Low Fat Veggie Bars 58

Fat Free Cream of Broccoli
Soup 84
Deliciously Different
Reduced Fat Broccoli
Salad 100

Bugs on a Log 62
Busy Mom's Low Fat Chicken
Pot Pie 147

C

Cakes
Stacey's Low Fat Coconut
Cake 200
Low Fat Devil's Food
Surprise 201
Low Fat Strawberry Cake
with Strawberry Dream
Icing 202
Fat Free Strawberry Dream
Icing 203
Low Fat Coffee Cake
204
Low Fat Blueberry Pound
Cake 205
Low Fat Apricot Nectar
Cake 206
Low Fat Apple Spice Cake
207
Light Lemon Cake 208
Fat Free Pear Cake 209
Low Fat Hummingbird
Cake 210
Low Fat Honey Bun Cake
211
Low Fat No Pound Cake
212
Low Fat Peach Cake 213
Low Fat Strawberry
Supreme Cake 214

Low Fat Sweet Potato Cake
215
No Sugar Added Pineapple
Surprise Cake 216
Punch Bowl Cake 217
Reduced Fat and Calorie
Turtle Cake 218
Reduced Fat Chocolate Chip
Pound Cake 219
Reduced Fat Chocolate Cola
Cake 220
Reduced Fat Mandarin
Orange Cake 221
Reduced Fat Poppy Seed
Cake 222
Reduced Fat Rum Cake 223
Reduced Fat "So Easy" Cake
224
Victoria & Elizabeth-Kate's
Reduced Fat Coke Float
Cake 225
Fat Free Banana Split Cake
226
Reduced Fat Ruston Peach
Cake 227
Reduced Fat King Cake
228
Reduced Fat Popcorn Cake
229
Working Woman's Easy
Rainbow Easter Cake 230
St. Patrick's Day Pistachio
Cake 232
Reduced Fat Strawberry
Sweetheart Cake 234
Reduced Fat Pumpkin Cake
236
Mardi Gras Cake 237
No Sugar Added Holiday
Peppermint Cake 238

Low Fat Chocolate Chip
Pumpkin Cake 239
Easter Bonnet Cake 240
Low Fat Icebox Fruit Cake
242
Easy Low Fat Cupcakes 243
No Sugar Added
Cheesecake 244
Low Fat Caramel-Pecan
Cheesecake 245

Chicken
Working Woman's Low Fat
Chicken and Dumplings
130
Reduced Fat Southwest
Chicken Casserole 131
Reduced Fat Poppy Seed
Chicken Casserole 132
Reduced Fat Mexican
Chicken & Dressing 133
Reduced Fat Mamaw's
Chicken Rice Bake 134
Reduced Fat King Ranch
Chicken 135
Reduced Fat Fettuccine
Alfredo 136
Reduced Fat Chicken
Almond Casserole 137
Reduced Fat Chicken
Roll-Ups 138
Reduced Fat Cheesy
Chicken Spectacular
139
Reduced Fat Almond
Chicken Stir-Fry 140
Mom's Day Out Crock Pot
Chicken Casserole 141
Low Fat White Chicken
Chili 142

Reduced Fat Cheesy Squash
143
Low Fat Mexican Casserole
144
Low Fat Chicken Rolls 145
Low Fat Chicken Ole
Casserole 146
Busy Mom's Low Fat
Chicken Pot Pie 147
Best Ever Low Fat Baked
Chicken 148
Low Fat Chicken Lagnaippe
149
Easy Low Fat Chicken
Cordon Bleu 150
Low Fat Cheesy Chicken
and Spaghetti 151
Low Fat Chicken Stuffed
Shells 152
Low Fat Mexican Pasta
153
Reduced Fat Chicken
Enchilada Pasta 154
Peach Glazed Cornish Hens
155
Orange Marmalade Cornish
Hens 156

Christmas In a Jar Mexican Dip
Mix 50
Christmas In a Jar Sugar Free
Spiced Tea 65
Christmas In a Jar Hot
Chocolate Mix 66
Christmas In a Jar Nine Bean
Soup Mix 74
Christmas in a Jar White
Christmas Bars 275
Cinnamon Bread Pudding with
Whiskey Sauce 302

Cookies
Low Fat Whippersnaps 260
Stacey's Low Fat Oatmeal &
Chocolate Chip Cookies
261
Chocolate Chip Spider Web
Cookie 262
Mardi Gras Cake Mix
Cookies 263
Light White Chocolate Chip
and Cranberry Cookies
264
Eggs In The Grass Boiled
Cookies 265
Low Fat French Vanilla
Cookies 266

Couscous with Shrimp 187

D
Deliciously Different Reduced
Fat Broccoli Salad 100

Desserts
I Can't Believe It's Low Fat
Homemade Ice Cream
(with Real Candy Bars)
276
Stacey's Fat Free No Sugar
Added Homemade Ice
Cream 277
No Sugar Added Fat Free
Sweet Potato Ice Cream
278
Fat Free Easy Ice Cream 279
Reduced Fat Blueberry
Delight 280
Easy Low Fat Blueberry
Cobbler 281
Fat Free Lemon Mousse 282

Low Fat Banana Pudding
283
Low Fat Turtle Trifle 284
Low Fat Four Layer Delight
285
Low Fat Hawaiian Delight
286
No Sugar Added Fresh
Tropical Fruit Trifle 287
No Sugar Added Strawberry
Trifle 288
Quick and Easy Low Fat
Strawberry Trifle Delight
289
Low Fat Fruit Pizza 290
Low Fat Halloween Trifle
291
Witches Hands 292
Low Fat Pumpkin Roll 293
Pumpkin Trifle 294
Low Fat Spooky Graveyard
Treat 296
Reduced Fat Spring Four-
Layer Delight 297
Reduced Fat "Reindeer
Food" 298
Low Fat Cranberry Fluff
299
Low Fat Christmas Bread
Pudding 300
Rum or Whiskey Sauce
301
Fat Free Rice Krispies
Holiday Treats 301
Cinnamon Bread Pudding
with Whiskey Sauce 302
Fat Free Cherries in the
Snow 303
Low Fat Graham Cracker
Crust 304

E

Easter Bonnet Cake 240

Easy Low Fat Blueberry Cobbler 281

Easy Low Fat Chicken Cordon Bleu 150

Easy Low Fat Cupcakes 243

Easy Low Fat Etouffee 195

Eggs In The Grass Boiled Cookies 265

Everybody's Favorite Spinach 118

F

Fat Free 5-Fruit Salad 106

Fat Free Banana Bread 112

Fat Free Banana Split Cake 226

Fat Free Cherries in the Snow 303

Fat Free Chicken Enchilada Dip 40

Fat Free Corn Dip 41

Fat Free Crabmeat Surprise Tray 60

Fat Free Cream of Broccoli Soup 84

Fat Free Easy Ice Cream 279

Fat Free Easy Shrimp Dip 52

Fat Free Fruit Salad 107

Fat Free Harvest Apple Muffins 116

Fat Free Lemon Mousse 282

Fat Free Nibblers 57

Fat Free Pear Cake 209

Fat Free Pistacho Salad 104

Fat Free Rice Krispies Holiday Treats 301

Fat Free Spectacular Spinach Dip 42

Fat Free Strawberry Dream Icing 203

Fat Free Stuffed Potatoes 120

Fat Free Tortilla Roll Ups 55

Fat Free Wassil 63

G

Ground Beef

Reduced Fat Taco Soup 76

Low Fat Taco Soup 79

Reduced fat Mexican Lasagna 159

Reduced Fat Tater Tot Casserole 160

Low Fat Hot Tamale Pie 161

Low Fat Baked Cabbage Jambalaya 162

Reduced Fat Slow Cooker Lasagna 163

Reduced Fat Meat and Cheese Pistolettes 164

Reduced Fat Pizza Pie 165

Reduced Fat Crescent Pizza Pie 166

Reduced Fat Chuck Wagon Chili Casserole 167

Reduced Fat Chili Spaghetti 168

Reduced Fat Chili Bake 169

Reduced Fat Cabbage Roll Casserole 170

Reduced Fat Beef & Salsa Burritos 171

Low Fat Speedy Taco bake 172

Low Fat Lasagna 173

Beef Noodle Casserole 174

H

Ham
Low Fat Ham Roll Ups 53
Low Fat Ham Delights 56
Low Fat Ham & Cheese
Biscuits 61
Hearty Low Fat Macaroni
Salad 94

I

I Can't Believe It's Low Fat
Homemade Ice Cream
(with Real Candy Bars) 276

L

Light Filet Mignon 176
Light Lemon Cake 208
Light Tuna Fish Salad 96
Light White Chocolate Chip and
Cranberry Cookies 264
Low Fat Apple Spice Cake
207
Low Fat Apricot Nectar Cake
206
Low Fat Baked Cabbage
Jambalaya 162
Low Fat Banana Pudding
283
Low Fat Black Bean Casserole
Ole 125
Low Fat Black Eye Cornbread
Casserole 158
Low Fat Blueberry Pound Cake
205
Low Fat Butterscotch Chocolate
Chip Bars 274
Low Fat Cappuccino Fudge
Brownie (Pumpkin Patch
Brownie, Spider Web &
Spooky Spiders) 272

Low Fat Caramel-Pecan
Cheesecake 245
Low Fat Cheesy Chicken and
Spaghetti 151
Low Fat Cheesy Seafood Bread
114
Low Fat Chess Squares 269
Low Fat Chicekn Rolls 145
Low Fat Chicken Florentine
Soup 81
Low Fat Chicken Lagnaippe 149
Low Fat Chicken Ole Casserole
146
Low Fat Chicken Spaghetti
Salad 92
Low Fat Chicken Stuffed Shells
152
Low Fat Chocolate Chip
Pumpkin Cake 239
Low Fat Christmas Bread
Pudding 300
Low Fat Coffee Cake 204
Low Fat Confetti-Pasta Salad 93
Low Fat Corn Casserole 126
Low Fat Cornbread Dressing
110
Low Fat Cranberry Fluff 299
Low Fat Crawfish Casserole 190
Low Fat Crawfish Enchiladas
189
Low Fat Creamy Artichoke and
Broccoli Dip 43
Low Fat Devil's Food Surprise
201
Low Fat Dip Chips 44
Low Fat Double Berry Spoon
Pie 247
Low Fat Exotic Chicken Salad
89
Low Fat Four Layer Delight 285

Low Fat French Vanilla Cookies 266
Low Fat Frozen Salad 105
Low Fat Fruit Pizza 290
Low Fat Fudge Brownies 268
Low Fat Graham Cracker Crust 304
Low Fat Halloween Trifle 291
Low Fat Ham & Cheese Biscuits 61
Low Fat Ham Delights 56
Low Fat Ham Roll Ups 53
Low Fat Hawaiian Bread 113
Low Fat Hawaiian Delight 286
Low Fat Hello Dollies 270
Low Fat Honey Bun Cake 211
Low Fat Hot Chicken Salad 90
Low Fat Hot Tamale Pie 161
Low Fat Hummingbird Cake 210
Low Fat Icebox Fruit Cake 242
Low Fat Jambalaya 186
Low Fat Lasagna 173
Low Fat Lemon Icebox Pie 249
Low Fat Louisiana Mud Pie 255
Low Fat Mexican Casserole 144
Low Fat Mexican Pasta 153
Low Fat Mexican Salad 101
Low Fat Mini Apple Pies 246
Low Fat No Pound Cake 212
Low Fat Orange Spooky Salad 103
Low Fat Oriental Chicken Salad 91
Low Fat Oven Stew 175
Low Fat Pasta and Fruit Chicken Salad 88
Low Fat Peach Cake 213
Low Fat Picante Rice with Fish 192
Low Fat Potato Casserole 127
Low Fat Potato Soup 80
Low Fat Pumpkin Roll 293
Low Fat Quick and Easy Corn Casserole 128
Low Fat Salmon Croquettes 179
Low Fat Seven-Layer Tex Mex Dip 45
Low Fat Speedy Taco bake 172
Low Fat Spicy Apple Muffins 115
Low Fat Spicy Chicken Quesadillas 54
Low Fat Spooky Graveyard Treat 296
Low Fat Strawberry Cake with Strawberry Dream Icing 202
Low Fat Strawberry Supreme Cake 214
Low Fat Sugar Free Lemon Berry Pie 248
Low Fat Sweet Potato Cake 215
Low Fat Taco Soup 79
Low Fat Three Bean & Wild Rice Casserole 124
Low Fat Triple Chocolate Valentine Brownies 271
Low Fat Tuna Cheese Salad 97
Low Fat Turtle Trifle 284
Low Fat Veggie Bars 58
Low Fat Venison Chili 196
Low Fat Whippersnaps 260
Low Fat White Chicken Chili 142

M

Mardi Gras Cake 237
Mardi Gras Cake Mix Cookies 263

Marshmallows
 Peanut Butter Squares 62
 Reduced Fat Popcorn Cake
  229
 Low Fat Icebox Fruit Cake
  242
 Low Fat Louisiana Mud Pie
  255
Modified Blueberry Salad 102
Mom's Day Out Crock Pot
 Chicken Casserole 141

N
Nantucket Crab 53
No Sugar Added Cheesecake
 244
No Sugar Added Double Layer
 Sweet Potato Pie 258
No Sugar Added Fat Free Sweet
 Potato Ice Cream 278
No Sugar Added Fresh Tropical
 Fruit Trifle 287
No Sugar Added Holiday
 Peppermint Cake 238
No Sugar Added Lemon Ice Box
 Pie 251
No Sugar Added Oreo Cookie
 Pie 259
No Sugar Added Pineapple
 Surprise Cake 216
No Sugar Added Strawberry
 Trifle 288

O
Orange Marmalade Cornish
 Hens 156

P
Party Chicken Salad 87
Peach Glazed Cornish Hens 155

Peanut Butter Squares
 62

Pies
 Low Fat Mini Apple Pies
  246
 Low Fat Double Berry
  Spoon Pie 247
 Low Fat Sugar Free Lemon
  Berry Pie 248
 Low Fat Lemon Icebox Pie
  249
 Reduced Fat Chilled Key
  Lime Pie 250
 No Sugar Added Lemon Ice
  Box Pie 251
 Reduced Fat Mom 's Fresh
  Peach Pie 252
 Reduced Fat Strawberry
  Cream Pie 253
 Sugar Free Blueberry Pie
  254
 Low Fat Louisiana Mud Pie
  255
 Reduced Fat and Calorie
  Pecan Pie 256
 Reduced Fat Fresh Sweet
  Potato Pie 257
 No Sugar Added Double
  Layer Sweet Potato Pie
  258
 No Sugar Added Oreo
  Cookie Pie 259

Pizza Squares 63

Pork
 Reduced Fat Pork Chop
  Casserole 178

Potatoes
Reduced Fat Cheesy Potato
Soup 77
Low Fat Potato Soup 80
Fat Free Stuffed Potatoes
120

Pumpkin Trifle 294
Punch Bowl Cake 217

Q
Quick and Easy Low Fat
Strawberry Trifle Delight 289

R
Raisins
Sugar Free Raisin Bars 267
Low Fat Christmas Bread
Pudding 300
Cinnamon Bread Pudding
with Whiskey Sauce 302

Red Hot Punch 64
Reduced Fat "Reindeer Food"
298
Reduced Fat "So Easy" Cake 224
Reduced Fat Almond Chicken
Stir-Fry 140
Reduced Fat and Calorie Pecan
Pie 256
Reduced Fat and Calorie Turtle
Cake 218
Reduced Fat Beef & Salsa
Burritos 171
Reduced Fat Blueberry Delight
280
Reduced Fat Breakfast Pizza
117
Reduced Fat Cabbage Roll
Casserole 170

Reduced Fat Cajun Shrimp Dip
49
Reduced Fat Catfish Parmesan
193
Reduced Fat Cheesy Chicken
Spectacular 139
Reduced Fat Cheesy Chili Dip
46
Reduced Fat Cheesy Crawfish
Dip 47
Reduced Fat Cheesy Green Bean
Casserole 123
Reduced Fat Cheesy Potato
Soup 77
Reduced Fat Cheesy Squash
143
Reduced Fat Chicken Almond
Casserole 137
Reduced Fat Chicken and
Sausage Gumbo 82
Reduced Fat Chicken Enchilada
Pasta 154
Reduced Fat Chicken Roll-Ups
138
Reduced Fat Chili Bake 169
Reduced Fat Chili Casserole 157
Reduced Fat Chili Spaghetti 168
Reduced Fat Chilled Key Lime
Pie 250
Reduced Fat Chocolate Chip
Pound Cake 219
Reduced Fat Chocolate Cola
Cake 220
Reduced Fat Chuck Wagon Chili
Casserole 167
Reduced Fat Cornbread Salad
109
Reduced Fat Crawfish Pie 188
Reduced Fat Crescent Pizza Pie
166

Reduced Fat Fettuccine Alfredo 136

Reduced Fat Fresh Sweet Potato Pie 257

Reduced Fat Hot Seafood Dip 48

Reduced Fat Island Salad 98

Reduced Fat King Cake 228

Reduced Fat King Ranch Chicken 135

Reduced Fat Macaroni and Cheese Soup 78

Reduced Fat Mamaw's Chicken Rice Bake 134

Reduced Fat Mandarin Orange Cake 221

Reduced Fat Mardi Gras Salad 99

Reduced Fat Meat and Cheese Pistolettes 164

Reduced Fat Mexican Chicken & Dressing 133

Reduced fat Mexican Lasagna 159

Reduced Fat Mexican Stew 197

Reduced Fat Mom 's Fresh Peach Pie 252

Reduced Fat Pizza Pie 165

Reduced Fat Popcorn Cake 229

Reduced Fat Poppy Seed Cake 222

Reduced Fat Poppy Seed Chicken Casserole 132

Reduced Fat Pork Chop Casserole 178

Reduced Fat Pumpkin Cake 236

Reduced Fat Rum Cake 223

Reduced Fat Ruston Peach Cake 227

Reduced Fat Seafood Enchiladas 184

Reduced Fat Seafood Spaghetti 183

Reduced Fat Shrimp Delight 182

Reduced Fat Slow Cooker Lasagna 163

Reduced Fat Southwest Chicken Casserole 131

Reduced Fat Southwestern Chicken Salad 86

Reduced Fat Spring Four-Layer Delight 297

Reduced Fat Strawberry Cream Pie 253

Reduced Fat Strawberry Sweetheart Cake 234

Reduced Fat Stuffed Catfish 191

Reduced Fat Stuffed Squash 119

Reduced Fat Sunburst Chicken Salad 85

Reduced Fat Taco Soup 76

Reduced Fat Tater Tot Casserole 160

Reduced Fat Tuna Casserole 180

Reduced Fat Wild Rice Soup 73

Rice

Low Fat Corn Casserole 126

Reduced Fat Mamaw's Chicken Rice Bake 134

Reduced Fat Cheesy Chicken Spectacular 139

Shrimp Etouffee 181

Rum or Whiskey Sauce 301

S

Salads

Reduced Fat Sunburst Chicken Salad 85

Reduced Fat Southwestern Chicken Salad 86

Party Chicken Salad 87

Low Fat Pasta and Fruit Chicken Salad 88

Low Fat Exotic Chicken Salad 89

Low Fat Hot Chicken Salad 90

Low Fat Oriental Chicken Salad 91

Low Fat Chicken Spaghetti Salad 92

Low Fat Confetti-Pasta Salad 93

Hearty Low Fat Macaroni Salad 94

Wonderful Low Fat Turkey Salad 95

Light Tuna Fish Salad 96

Low Fat Tuna Cheese Salad 97

Reduced Fat Island Salad 98

Reduced Fat Mardi Gras Salad 99

Deliciously Different Reduced Fat Broccoli Salad 100

Low Fat Mexican Salad 101

Modified Blueberry Salad 102

Low Fat Orange Spooky Salad 103

Fat Free Pistacho Salad 104

Low Fat Frozen Salad 105

Fat Free 5-Fruit Salad 106

Fat Free Fruit Salad 107

Yogurt Fruit Dressing 108

Reduced Fat Cornbread Salad 109

Seafood

Low Fat Salmon Croquettes 179

Reduced Fat Tuna Casserole 180

Shrimp Etouffee 181

Reduced Fat Shrimp Delight 182

Reduced Fat Seafood Spaghetti 183

Reduced Fat Seafood Enchiladas 184

Low Fat Jambalaya 186

Couscous with Shrimp 187

Reduced Fat Crawfish Pie 188

Low Fat Crawfish Enchiladas 189

Low Fat Crawfish Casserole 190

Reduced Fat Stuffed Catfish 191

Low Fat Picante Rice with Fish 192

Reduced Fat Catfish Parmesan 193

Catfish Courtbouillion 194

Easy Low Fat Etouffee 195

Side Dishes

Reduced Fat Breakfast Pizza 117

Everybody's Favorite
Spinach 118
Reduced Fat Stuffed Squash
119
Fat Free Stuffed Potatoes
120
Sweet Potato Yum Yum
Casserole 121
Victoria's Favorite Casserole
122
Reduced Fat Cheesy Green
Bean Casserole 123
Low Fat Quick and Easy
Corn Casserole 128
Low Fat Three Bean & Wild
Rice Casserole 124
Low Fat Black Bean
Casserole Ole 125
Low Fat Corn Casserole 126
Low Fat Potato Casserole
127

Soups
Southwest Vegetable Soup
72
Reduced Fat Wild Rice Soup
73
Christmas In a Jar Nine
Bean Soup Mix 74
Reduced Fat Taco Soup 76
Reduced Fat Cheesy Potato
Soup 77
Reduced Fat Macaroni and
Cheese Soup 78
Low Fat Taco Soup 79
Low Fat Potato Soup 80
Low Fat Chicken Florentine
Soup 81
Reduced Fat Chicken and
Sausage Gumbo 82

Fat Free Cream of Broccoli
Soup 84

St. Patrick's Day Pistachio Cake
232
Stacey's Fat Free Mexican
Cornbread 111
Stacey's Fat Free No Sugar
Added Homemade Ice Cream
277
Stacey's Low Fat Coconut Cake
200
Stacey's Low Fat Oatmeal &
Chocolate Chip Cookies 261

Strawberries
Strawberry Yogurt Smoothie
68
Low Fat Strawberry Cake
with Strawberry Dream
Icing 202
No Sugar Added Strawberry
Trifle 288
Quick and Easy Low Fat
Strawberry Trifle Delight
289
Strawberry Yogurt Smoothie 68

Sugar Free Blueberry Pie 254
Sugar Free Punch 67
Sugar Free Raisin Bars 267
Sweet Potato Yum Yum
Casserole 121

T
Turkey
Reduced Fat Chili Casserole
157
Low Fat Black Eye
Cornbread Casserole 158

V

Venison
Low Fat Venison Chili 196
Reduced Fat Mexican Stew
197

Victoria & Elizabeth-Kate's
Reduced Fat Coke Float Cake
225
Victoria's Favorite Casserole
122

W

Witches Hands 292
Wonderful Low Fat Turkey
Salad 95
Working Woman's Easy
Rainbow Easter Cake 230
Working Woman's Low Fat
Chicken and Dumplings 130

Y

Yogurt Fruit Dressing 108
Yogurt Fruit Dressing 59